CW00500632

THE PONY CLUB

The Worldwide Association of Young Riders

Patron: HRH The Princess Royal, KG KT GCVO QSO GCL
President: The Lady Lloyd Webber
Life Vice Presidents: Mary Anderson, Robin Danielli, Lt Col. Tadzik Kopanski
Chairman: Tim Vestey
Chief Executive: Marcus Capel

The Pony Club is an international voluntary youth organisation for those interested in horses, ponies and riding. It is the largest association of riders in the world. It is represented in no less than 27 countries and has a membership exceeding 110,000.

THE PONY CLUB HANDBOOK IS PUBLISHED BY THE PONY CLUB

Lowlands Equestrian Centre, Old Warwick Road, Warwick, CV35 7AX

Tel: 02476 698300
Email: enquiries@pcuk.org
Website: pcuk.org

Registered Charity No. **1050146**
Incorporated as a Company Limited by Guarantee
Registered in England No. **3072475**

Contents

Handbook Version: 22.1.5

PONY CLUB TEST
C
pcuk.org
FIRE SAFETY
pcuk.org
pcuk.org
ROAD RIDER
pcuk.org
FUNDRAISING
pcuk.org
CARE OF THE FOOT
pcuk.org
PONY CLUB TEST
C+
pcuk.org

Pony Club Committee Structure

Term of office ends at the end of year in brackets after each person's name.

TRUSTEES

Tim Vestey
(Chairman) (2023)
chairman@pcuk.org

Clare Valori (Vice Chairman) (2023)

Andrew James (2022)

Deborah Custance-Baker (AR) (2022)

Elizabeth Lowry (AR) (2023)

Philip Freedman (2023)

Justine Baynes (2023)

Nigel Howlett (Treasurer) (2023)

MANAGEMENT COMMITTEE

Clare Valori (Chairman) (2023)

Louly Thornycroft (AR) (2024)

Andrew Tulloch (AR) (2024)

Sarah MacDonald (Training)

Nigel Howlett (Treasurer)

Pleasance Jewitt (Area Representatives)

Rosalind Slinger (Centre Membership)

Paul Darby (HSS and Horse Welfare)

Helen Griffiths (Sports)

Helen Jackson Volunteers & Officials)

Andrew James (Rules & Compliance)

Marcus Capel (CEO)

Heidi Lockyer (Deputy CEO)

Sue Woolnough (Finance Manager)

FINANCE & RISK COMMITTEE

Nigel Howlett
(Chairman and Treasurer) (2023)

Patrick Campbell (AR) (2024)
Sue Woolnough (Finance Manager)
Tim Vestey (Trustee) (2023)
Helen Jackson (AR) (2024)
Isobel Mills (2022)
TBC (Risk)

TRAINING COMMITTEE

Sarah MacDonald FBHS
(Chairman) (2024)
trainingchairman@pcuk.org

Catherine Cawdron (2022)
Vicki Macdonald (2022)
Paul Tapner (2022)
Marie Ryan (2022)
Hetta Wilkinson (AR) (2022)
Karen Harris (AR) (2024)
Janet Douglas (2022)
Carole Broad FBHS (2022)
Dr Will Harrison (2022)
Henry Church-Huxley (Member Representative) (2022)

Ex-Officio Members:
Pleasance Jewitt (AR Chairman)
Clare Valori (Vice Chairman)
Helen Griffiths (Sports Chairman)
Rosalind Slinger (Centre Chairman)

CENTRE MEMBERSHIP COMMITTEE

Rosalind Slinger (Chairman) (2022)
centrechairman@pcuk.org

Rosemary Clarke (Overseas Representative) (2024)
Sheila Clifford (AR) (2024)
Amelia Morris-Payne (2024)
Natalie O'Rourke (2022)
Sara Tremlett (AR) (2024)
Hilary Wakefield (2022)
Lea Allen (2022)
Katy Powell (2022)
Di Pegrum (2024)

HEALTH AND SAFETY, SAFEGUARDING AND HORSE WELFARE ADVISORY COMMITTEE

Paul Darby (Chairman) (2024)
safety@pcuk.org

Dr Ted Adams (2022)
Ben Mayes (2022)
Christine Gould (2024)
Sandra Fisher (2022)
Hazel Warburton (2024)
Abby Bernard (A.R.) (2023)
Clare Valori
TBC (AR)

RULES AND COMPLIANCE COMMITTEE

Andrew James (Chairman) (2024)
rcchairman@pcuk.org

Maureen Costello (Ex Officio) (2024)
Rosalind Slinger (2024)
Christina Thompson (2024)
Louly Thornycroft (AR) (2024)
Clare Valori (Ex Officio)
Hazel Warburton (Ex Officio) (2024)
Heidi Lockyer (Deputy CEO)
Karen Harris (A.R.) (2024)
Emma Holliwell (Ex Officio)

VOLUNTEERS AND OFFICIALS COMMITTEE

Helen Jackson (Chairman) (2022)
volunteerschairman@pcuk.org

Catriona Willison (2024)
Liz Lowry (AR) (2024)
Helen Jackson (AR) (2024)
Maureen Costello (2024)
Tim Vestey (ex officio)
Hazel Warburton (2024)
Heidi Lockyer (Deputy CEO)
Diane Pegrum (2024)
Emma Neal (2024)
Clare Valori (Ex Officio)

AREA REPRESENTATIVES

Pleasance Jewitt (Chairman) (2024)
area9@pcuk.org

AREA 1
Catriona Willison (2022)
area1@pcuk.org
01360 860257 / 07979 735274

AREA 2
Sheila Clifford (2022)
area2@pcuk.org
0191 388 3756

AREA 3
Nicky Morrison (2022)
area3@pcuk.org
01677 450998

AREA 4
Robin Bower (2023)
area4@pcuk.org
07976 272272

AREA 5
Andrew Tulloch (2024)
area5@pcuk.org
07831 315104

AREA 6
Patrick Campbell (2024)
area6@pcuk.org
07801 423898

AREA 7
Andrew James (2024)
area7@pcuk.org
01455 291273 / 07737 877697

AREA 8
Hetta Wilkinson (2024)
area8@pcuk.org
07880 728708 / 01206 330476

AREA 9
Pleasance Jewitt (2024)
area9@pcuk.org
01285 821715

AREA 10
Isobel Mills (2024)
area10@pcuk.org
07976 779140

AREA 11
Abby Bernard (2022)
area11@pcuk.org
07775 712512

AREA 12
Helen Jackson (2022)
area12@pcuk.org
01494 881321 / 07941 818738

AREA 13
Sara Tremlett (2022)
area13@pcuk.org
01798.817476

AREA 14
Louly Thornycroft (2024)
area14@pcuk.org
01258 860614

AREA 15
Deborah Custance-Baker (2022)
area15@pcuk.org
01392 861750 / 07889 260446

AREA 16
Karen Harris (2022)
area16@pcuk.org
01548 857617 / 07470 366000

AREA 17
Liz Lowry (2022)
area17@pcuk.org
02891 870766

AREA 18
Julie Hodson (2024)
area18@pcuk.org
01239 654314

AREA 19
Anne Ekin (2024)
area19@pcuk.org
07711 630433

CENTRE COORDINATORS

Ros Slinger (Chairman) (2022)
centrechairman@pcuk.org

REA 1
drian Macleod
ea1.centres@pcuk.org
866 631875

REA 2
rah Lewins
ea2.centres@pcuk.org
799 404246

REA 3
nily Massey
ea3.centres@pcuk.org
826 430047

REA 4
hn Gilbert
ea4.centres@pcuk.org
7837 597561

REA 5
hn Gilbert
ea5.centres@pcuk.org
7837 597561

REA 6
nelia Morris-Payne
ea6.centres@pcuk.org
7816 955757

REA 7
aren Hudson
ea7.centres@pcuk.org
7974 182664

AREA 8
Diane Pegrum
area8.centres@pcuk.org
07890 919558

AREA 9
Lea Allen
area9.centres@pcuk.org
07801 278785

AREA 10
Lea Allen
area10.centres@pcuk.org
07801 278785

AREA 11
Sarah Glynn-Brooks
area11.centres@pcuk.org
07816 784487

AREA 12
Diane Pegrum
area12.centres@pcuk.org
07890 919558

AREA 13
Sally Blackmore
area13.centres@pcuk.org
07442 530080

AREA 14
Sara Greenwood
area14.centres@pcuk.org
07773 782052

AREA 15
TBC
area15.centres@pcuk.org

AREA 16
Helen Moore
area16.centres@pcuk.org
07828 837784

AREA 17
TBC
area17.centres@pcuk.org

AREA 18
Lea Allen
area18.centres@pcuk.org
07801 278785

AREA 19
Lea Allen
area19.centres@pcuk.org
07801 278785

AREA 20 (Overseas)
Rosemary Clarke
overseas.centres@pcuk.org
07729 016978

SPORTS

DRESSAGE

Helen Griffiths
(Chairman) (2024)
dressagechairman@pcuk.org

Karen Burner (2024)
Cathy Burrell (2024)
Sheila Clifford (AR) (2022)
Sue Coombe-Tennant (2024)
Rachael Coulter (2024)
Isobel Mills (AR) (2024)
Rory Howard (2024)
Linda Pearce (2024)

EVENTING

Charlotte Rowell
(Chairman) (2024)
eventingchairman@pcuk.or

Catie Baird (2024)
Nicky Morrison (AR) (2022)
David Merrett (2022)
Christina Thompson (2024)
Catriona Willison (AR) (2022)
Patrick Campbell (2022)
Sarah Verney (2022)

ENDURANCE

Robert Blane
(Chairman) (2024)
endurancechairman@pcuk.org

Rosemary Attfield (2022)
Deborah Custance-Baker (AR) (2024)
Emma Moffat (2022)
Fiona Williams (2024)
Tom Eaton-Evans (2024)
Amanda Barton (2024)

MOUNTED GAMES

Ian Mariner
(Chairman) (2024)
mgchairman@pcuk.org

Alison Bell (2024)
Rowley Boulton (2022)
Marcus Capel (2024)
Tracey Cooksley (2024)
Vicky Dungait (2022)
Pennie Drummond (2024)
Marian Harding (2024)
Carol Howsam (2022)
Andrew James (AR) (2024)
Liz Lowry (AR) (2024)
Catriona Willison (2024)

POLO

Charles Whittington (Chairman) (2022)
polochairman@pcuk.org

enny Blake Thomas (2024)
:hris Eaton (2024)
illy Emerson (2022)
leasance Jewitt (AR) (2022)
Bethan Hitchman (2024)
Brig. Christopher Price (2024)
Brig. Justin Stanhope-White (2022)
Sara Tremlett (AR) (2022)
o Whittington (2024)
Beverly Nicholls (2024)

POLOCROSSE

Iain Heaton
(Chairman) (2022)
pxchairman@pcuk.org

Caro Daniels (2022)
Liz Lowry (AR) (2024)
Natalie Harpin (2022)
Hetta Wilkinson (AR) (2024)
Ian Whitehead (2022)
Pam Drew (2024)

PONY RACING

Charles Barnett
(Chairman) (2022)
racingchairman@pcuk.org

Maureen Costello (2024)
Nicky Morrison (AR) (2022)
Ruth Hurley (2024)
Sara Tremlett (AR) (2024)
Louise Shepherd (2024)
Jane Clark (2024)

SHOW JUMPING

James Loffet
(Chairman) (2022)
sjchairman@pcuk.org

Hannah Jackson (2022)
Judy Edwards (2022)
Kirsty Hardstaff (2024)
Liz Lowry (2024)
Nicky Morrison (AR) (2024)
Hetta Wilkinson (AR) (2024)
Jane Ogle (2024)

TETRATHLON

Mandy Donaldson
(Chairman) (2023)
tetchairman@pcuk.org

Bee Bell (2024)
Jayne Bowman (2024)
Nick Cripps (2024)
Meg Green (2024)
Heather Greenslade (2022)
Judy Hardcastle (2022)
Julie Hodson (AR) (2024)
Rory Howard (2024)
Richard Mosley (Co-ordinator Representative) (2022)
Zoe Kennerley (2022)
Louly Thornycroft (AR) (2024)
Liz Wilkinson (Co-ordinator Chairman) (2024)

BRANCH OPERATIONS DIRECTORS

Maureen Costello (2024) – bod1@pcuk.org
Hazel Warburton (2024) – bod3@pcuk.org

For full details of The Pony Club Governance Structure visit pcuk.org

Rules of The Pony Club

(Text in bold type and sidelined denotes a change from the Rules as printed in the 2021 Handbook)

Any changes made to the Rules of The Pony Club during the year will be made available online at pcuk.org and Branches and Centres will be notified.

1. INTRODUCTION

Purpose

1.1 The Pony Club is a voluntary youth organisation for young people interested in ponies and riding. It is a Registered Charity and is subject to Charity legislation and to regulation by the Charity Commission. The Legal Objects of The Pony Club are set out in clause 4 of the Articles of Association (a copy of which may be obtained from The Pony Club Office upon payment of a fee).

The purpose of The Pony Club is:

- To promote and advance the education and understanding of the public and particularly children and young people, in all matters relating to horsemanship and the horse.
- To encourage the development of sportsmanship, unlocking potential by building resilience, confidence, teamwork and leadership skills.
- To support and develop the volunteering network to strengthen The Pony Club community and sustain life-long engagement with equestrianism.

1.2 The Pony Club Office is at **Lowlands Equestrian Centre, Old Warwick Road, Warwick, CV35 7AX** from where The Pony Club is managed by a permanent staff responsible to the governing body (the Trustees).

Health and Safety Policy

1.3 The Trustees are committed to ensuring so far as is reasonably practicable, the Health and Safety of its employees, of everyone who assists The Pony Club, in whatever capacity. Members and their families and members of the public who may be affected by the activities of The Pony Club.

1.4 The Trustees will ensure that management procedures and rules are in place to ensure that all Pony Club activities ar run with due regard for the Health and Safety of all those people who may be affected by those activities and to ensure that all statutory duties are met.

1.5 Each employee, Area Representative, and District Commissioner/Centre Proprietor shall be given such information, instruction and training as is necessary for them to perform their duties in safety. When tasks require particular skills additional to those of The Pony Club staff and volunteers, a competent person or contractor with the necessary experience and training shall be engaged.

1.6 Each employee and volunteer will be expected to co-operate with The Pony Club or District Commissioner/Centre Proprietor to ensure that all statutory duties are complied with and to ensure that all work activities are carried out safely. Each individual has a legal obligation to take reasonable care for his or her own Health and Safety, and for the safety of others who may be affected by his or her acts or omissions. Any person who is concerned about any issue relating to Health and Safety should raise the matter with their District Commissioner or manager at the earliest available opportunity.

Organisational Arrangements

1.7 The Chief Executive and the Pony Club Office shall on behalf of the Trustees

i. Ensure that Rules and procedures are published and updated regularly to cover all Pony Club activities;
ii. Ensure that adequate Employer's Liability and Public Liability insurance cover, as determined by The Trustees of The Pony Club, is obtained;
iii. Ensure that adequate training and instruction is provided for Area Representatives, District Commissioners, Volunteers and Employees;
iv. Maintain a central record of competent Coaches and their attendance at professional development training. Coaches may be deemed to be competent by virtue of qualification, achievement or experience in one or more fields relevant to Pony Club activities;
v. Ensure that all activities organised by The Pony Club are run with due regard to the Health and Safety of everyone who may be affected by that activity;
vi. Ensure that adequate safeguarding procedures are notified to Area Representatives, District Commissioners and Centre Proprietors for implementation at all Pony Club activities;
vii. Maintain effective communications on Health and Safety issues with employees, Area Representatives, District Commissioners and Centre Proprietors;
viii. Require accidents to be investigated to identify the causes so that actions may be taken to reduce the possibility of a recurrence.

1.8 District Commissioners shall operate their Branches in accordance with the Rules of The Pony Club and statutory requirements and with due regard for the health and safety of their Members, parents and guardians, volunteers and any other person who may be affected by the activities organised by the Branch.

1.9 Area Representatives are responsible for monitoring the Health and Safety performance of the Branches in their area.

1.10 Pony Club Centres are responsible for their own Health and Safety arrangements. These will be monitored by their Area Centre Coordinator and reported to The Pony Club Office as part of the Centre annual visit.

Responsibilities of Employees, Officials, Volunteers, Coaches and Contractors

1.11 All persons acting on behalf of The Pony Club or carrying out work for The Pony Club must -

i. Take reasonable care for their own Health and Safety;
ii. Consider the safety of other persons who may be affected by their acts or omissions;
iii. Work within the limits of their own training and competence and the information and instructions they have received;
iv. Refrain from intentionally misusing or recklessly interfering with any equipment provided for Health and Safety reasons;
v. Report any hazardous defects in plant and equipment or shortcomings in the existing safety arrangements to a member of the Branch Committee, or their immediate Pony Club contact, as soon as practicable;
vi. Report all accidents to a member of the Branch Committee, or their immediate Pony Club contact.

1.12 Health and Safety is to be given priority

over any other Pony Club activity.

Other Legislation

1.13 It is also the policy of The Pony Club to take account of, and to implement as required, legislation on human rights, legislation which impacts voluntary youth organisations, and which regulates the care and supervision of young people.

1.14 In relation to equity, equality and diversity, The Pony Club

i. aims to ensure that all people, irrespective of race, gender, ability, ethnic origin, social status or sexual orientation have equal opportunities to take part in equestrianism at all levels and in any roles;
ii. seeks to educate and guide Pony Club Members, their employees and volunteers on the ownership, adoption and implementation of its Equity, Equality and Diversity Action Plan;
iii. intends to raise awareness of equity, equality and diversity through the implementation of this policy and the adoption of the Equity, Equality and Diversity Action Plan; and, as a result of this process
iv. aims to monitor, review and evaluate progress in achieving the stated aims and objectives and to feed back to member bodies on progress made.

1.15 The Pony Club will ensure that its recruitment and selection procedures are fair, transparent and meet the appropriate legal requirements.

2. DEFINITIONS

2.1 In these Rules:

"Area" means a geographic sub-division of Great Britain and Northern Ireland.

"Area Centre Coordinator" means the person responsible for supporting Centres within an Area and for advising on Centre Membershi issues within that Area.

"Area Representative" means the person responsible for overseeing Pony Club activiti within an Area.

"BETA" means the British Equestrian Trade Association.

"BEF" means the British Equestrian.

"Branch" means an operating sub-division o The Pony Club, organising Pony Club activiti at a local level.

"Branch Member" means a Member of a Branch.

"Branch Operations Director" means a perso appointed by the Management Committee to assist relationships and communication, when required, between Branches and Area Representatives, and the Pony Club Office, and also to mediate in inter-Branch o intra-Branch disputes. He will be appointed for 3 years but may offer himself for re-appointment.

"Centre Member" includes both a Centre Member and a Centre Plus Member unless the context otherwise requires and means someone who is a Member through a Pony Club Centre.

"Centre Membership Scheme" means the scheme for the approval of riding establishments as a Pony Club Centre administered by The Pony Club Office for the membership of Centre Members.

"Centre Plus Member" means someone who is a Member through a Pony Club Centre wh has regular access to ride a horse/pony outsi of Centre organised activities. This includes someone who owns, leases or borrows a hors pony.

"Championships" means The Pony

Club Championships. Including where the context requires the Pony Club Tetrathlon Championships, The Pony Club Polo Championships and the Regional Championships.

"Charity" means "The Pony Club" as constituted as a Registered Charity.

"Children of the Family" includes siblings, half siblings, adopted children, foster children, and children who have a guardian residing at their address.

"Company Member" means a person who is entitled to vote at general meetings of The Pony Club being the Trustees, the Area Representatives, the Branch Operations Directors and the Chairmen of all National Committees.

"Designated Funds" are funds that have been earmarked by the Trustees or by a Branch Committee including where the context requires the Regional Championships the Pony Club Tetrathlon Championships and the Pony Club Polo Championships for specific projects.

"District Commissioner" means the person responsible for administering Pony Club activities within a Branch.

"Equestrian Professional" means a person who is financially interested in letting out or selling horses, in instructing in equitation or keeping liveries or other equestrian facilities.

"Family Membership" means membership available for up to a maximum of 5 Children of the Family living at the same permanent address who are Members of the same Branch.

"Free reserves" are the assets of the Branch (excluding fixed assets) less its liabilities and less any Restricted or Designated Funds.

"Handbook" means the annual publication giving information about The Pony Club.

"he" means either he or she and "his" means either his or her.

"Health and Safety Policy" means the Policy as stated in the introduction to these Rules.

"Management Committee" means the executive body responsible for the day-to-day operation of The Pony Club, whose membership is defined in Rule 4.10.

"Member" includes a Branch Member and a Centre Member unless the context otherwise requires.

"Membership Subscription Year" means the period of twelve months commencing on the date the Member's subscription is paid and terminating on the day before the anniversary of this date.

"Non-Riding Member" means a Branch Member who is eligible to take part only in unmounted Pony Club activities (e.g. Horse and Pony Care, Quiz, Triathlon and unmounted rallies).

"Parents" shall include individuals with parental responsibility.

"Pony" means either a pony or a horse, except where the terminology is clearly specific to a pony.

"Pony Club Centre" or "Centre" means a Riding Centre that has been accepted to participate in the Centre Membership Scheme as a Pony Club Linked Riding Centre.

"Pony Club Office" or "The Office" means the central office maintained by The Pony Club, which is also the registered address of The Pony Club.

"Pony Club Year" means the period from 1 January to the following 31 December.

"Restricted Funds" are monies that have been given by a donor with conditions on how they are to be spent.

"Riding Member" means a Branch Member who is eligible to take part in all Pony Club activities whether mounted or unmounted.

"Rules" and "Rules of The Pony Club" mean the Rules of The Pony Club, as published in the Handbook, and displayed on the website. The Rules are determined by the Trustees (in the spirit and best interests of The Pony Club and its objectives). The Rules may be added to, cancelled in whole or in part or altered, as the Trustees or the Company Members at a general meeting deem necessary. The Trustees may also make temporary rules for a limited period. Changes or additions to the Rules will be published on the website. Any query about the operation of the Rules or request for clarification should be referred to the Trustees.

"Website" means the website of The Pony Club, available at pcuk.org

2.2 For the purposes of these Rules and individual sports rule books, a horse or pony shall be deemed to reach the age of 1 on the 1st January following the date on which it is foaled and shall be deemed to become a year older on each successive 1st January.

3. PERIOD OF OFFICE

3.1 The Chairman, Vice-Chairman and Treasurer shall serve in that capacity for a maximum of two terms of 3 years. No Trustee may serve for more than three consecutive terms of three years. They may then stand again after a period of 3 years has elapsed, up to a maximum of a further three consecutive terms of three years.

3.2 In exceptional circumstances, the Trustees may agree to an extension for a person who otherwise would have to retire, but for a maximum of 1 year.

3.3 This Rule shall prevail if it is in conflict with any other Rule.

4. STRUCTURE

The Trustees

4.1 The Trustees are the ultimate authority of The Pony Club (subject to review by the Company Members at the Annual General Meeting) and are responsible for the general administration and management of the affairs of The Pony Club. The Trustees may delegate their authority to subsidiary bodies, officials and employees. A register shall be maintained of all delegations and authority limits.

4.2 Reporting to the Trustees will be the Management Committee, the Finance Committee, the Health and Safety and Safeguarding Advisory Committee and the Chief Executive.

4.3 The Chairman of The Pony Club will be nominated by the Trustees after consultation with the Volunteers and Officials Committee. The Trustees' nomination will then be subject to confirmation by the Company Members at the Annual General Meeting. The Chairman will hold office for three years from 1st January after his appointment and, subject to Rule 3, a retiring Chairman will be eligible for re-appointment. The Trustees will also appoint a Vice Chairman of The Pony Club after a similar process of consultation, to assist the Chairman in the performance of his duties. The Vice Chairman shall have the same length of term of office as the Chairman.

4.4 If the appointed Chairman or Vice Chairman is an Area Representative or Sports Chairman, he will resign his original position.

4.5 The Chairman of the Area Representatives' Committee and the

Chairman of the Centre Membership Committee cannot be a Trustee whilst holding that position.

Honorary Appointments

4.6 The Trustees may make honorary appointments, such as President, or Vice President. The holders of such appointments will not, by virtue solely of that office, be members of any Pony Club Committee.

Finance Committee

4.7 The Finance Committee will monitor the integrity of The Pony Club's financial statements and internal controls. It will also review the budgets, the statutory accounts and the risk management systems, and will report on these to the Trustees at each meeting (so far as applicable). The Committee will also make recommendations to the Trustees in relation to the appointment and remuneration of the auditors and will have as specific terms of reference to

- oversee the financial reporting and disclosure process.
- monitor the choice of accounting policies and principles.
- oversee the hiring and performance and independence of the external auditors
- monitor internal controls and compliance with laws and regulations
- oversee preparation of the Trustees' annual report
- monitor the collation and updating of the risk register
- oversee the implementation of best anti-fraud practices
- oversee the implementation of appropriate whistle blowing practices
- implement and manage an appropriate board review process

4.8 The Committee will meet separately with the external auditors to discuss matters that the committee or auditors believe should be discussed privately and will be chaired by the Treasurer and shall include the Treasurer, another Trustee, two members nominated by the Area Representatives, and such other persons of appropriate expertise as may be nominated by the Trustees. The Committee will meet as required, but at least twice each year, and the Finance Manager (or other member of staff nominated by the Chief Executive) shall attend each meeting.

Management Committee

4.9 The Management Committee is the executive body charged with the management of The Pony Club in accordance with the policies and guidelines established by the Trustees and for the avoidance of doubt will be responsible for determining any matters which do not fall to be determined by any other committee.

4.10 The Vice Chairman of The Pony Club will chair the Management Committee and its membership will be:

- The Vice Chairman
- The Chairman of the Training Committee
- The Chairman of the Health and Safety and Safeguarding Advisory Committee
- The Chairman of the Centre Membership Committee
- The Chairman of the Area Representatives' Committee
- The Chairman of the Chairmen of the Sports Committee
- The Chairman of the Rules and Compliance Committee
- The Chairman of the Finance Committee
- The Chairman of the Volunteers and Officials Committee
- Two members elected by the Area Representatives
- The Chief Executive Officer
- The Finance Manager
- **The Deputy Chief Executive Officer**

4.11 Other members of the staff of The Pony Club may attend the meetings at the invitation of the Chairman of the Management Committee.

4.12 The elected Area Representatives will serve for a period of three years. When required, an election for a new Area Representative member of the Management Committee will be held at the last meeting in the year of the Area Representatives' Committee, with the appointment to be effective from the following 1st January. Each member of the Management Committee shall have a nominated substitute who shall be entitled in the absence of that member to attend the Management Committee in his stead.

4.13 It will not normally be appropriate for a member of the Management Committee who is not a member of staff to hold the same position for more than three consecutive terms of three years but he may stand again after a period of one year has elapsed to a maximum of a further three consecutive terms of three years.

4.14 An Area Representative serving as an elected Area Representative Trustee may not simultaneously serve on the Management Committee.

4.15 The Chairman of the Chairmen of Sports Committee will serve for a period of three years and may not immediately stand for re-election.

4.16 The Management Committee will meet at regular intervals.

4.17 Management Committee decisions will normally be made by open vote. However, the Management Committee may decide to have a secret ballot if a majority of those present so wish. All members will have equality of voting on all matters. The Chairman of the Management Committee will have the casting vote in the event of equality of votes A quorum will consist of not fewer than five members of the Management Committee entitled to vote.

Rules applicable to all committees

4.18 Unless specifically provided for elsewhere in these rules, the following Rules shall apply to all committees, with the exception of the Appeals Committee: -

4.19 Each committee shall have a chairman who will normally hold office for three years, terminating at the end of the third Pony Club Year, although he may offer himself for re-appointment.

4.20 Nominations for the Chairman can be made by the relevant Committee members and by Company Members. If more than one nomination is received, the relevant Committee members and the Company Members will vote on the appointment.

4.21 If the chairman of any committee loses the confidence of his committee members, and he is unwilling to resign, then this should be reported to the Management Committee in writing, signed by a majority of the committee members. The Management Committee will appoint a person to investigate fully and, if necessary, report back on the facts. The Management Committee, in its absolute discretion, may er the appointment of a committee chairman or any other committee member at any time upon giving written notice to the individual. The Management Committee will normally seek representations from the individual concerned and will normally give reasons for its decision.

4.22 Persons appointed to committees established under these rules are expected to contribute fully to the working of that committee and therefore any persons who, without reasonable excuse, fails to attend (either in person or by conference call) three consecutive meetings of the committee shall cease to be a member of that committee.

4.23 Each committee shall include up to two Area Representatives. Every eligible Area Representative shall be offered a place on at least one committee. Area Representatives will serve on a committee for three Pony Club Years. Other than in exceptional circumstances an Area Representative will not be eligible for re-appointment in their capacity as Area Representatives but may be appointed as an ordinary member of the committee.

4.24 Unless the Chairman of the Management Committee approves the appointment or that person is already a member of such a committee, a newly appointed Area Representative shall not be eligible for appointment to a committee until he has served for one complete Pony Club Year as an Area Representative. No later than 1st August each year, each Area Representative other than any such newly appointed Area Representative, shall be invited to indicate, the committees on which he wishes to serve. These should be given in order of preference. The Management Committee shall then allocate the Area Representatives to committees.

4.25 Other than the Area Representatives, persons will be invited to become members of committees because of their expertise in a particular area. They will serve for a period of three years but may offer themselves for re-election. All vacancies must be advertised on The Pony Club website. All candidates must be nominated in writing by a Company Member. If there are more nominations than there are places available, then a vote will be held. Those entitled to vote will be the existing members of the Committee, both continuing and retiring, and the Company members.

4.26 A list of the proposed composition of each committee for the coming year shall be submitted to the Annual General Meeting for ratification.

4.27 Proposals to fill casual vacancies shall be submitted to the next Management Committee meeting after the vacancy arises.

4.28 All members of a committee shall have equal voting rights, except that co-opted advisors shall not have a vote. The chairman of the committee shall have the casting vote in the event of equality of votes. Any three members of a committee will form a quorum.

Area Representatives' Committee

4.29 The Area Representatives' Committee will be chaired by an elected Area Representative and will meet at least twice a year. The voting members of the committee will be the 19 Area Representatives. The Branch Operations Directors shall be entitled to attend meetings of the committee but shall not have a vote.

Appeals Committee

4.30 In the event that any matter cannot be resolved by the Area Representatives, the Area Centre Coordinators, the Branch Operations Directors, the Management Committee, the Centre Membership Committee or the relevant Sport Committee, the Chairman of the Management Committee will establish a committee of three or more Company Members, retired Area Representatives or retired Chairmen of a Sports Committee at least one of whom must be an Area Representative. The committee will choose one of their number to act as chairman. The members chosen must not have a conflict of interest.

4.31 The Chairman will have the casting vote in the event of equality of votes.

4.32 The decisions of the Appeals Committee shall be final.

4.33 Any three members of the Appeals Committee will form a quorum.

Sport Committees

4.34 There shall be formed a committee for each Sport comprising **of up to** two Area Representatives plus other persons with knowledge and experience of each sport. The committee will in each case have responsibility for the administration of their sport within The Pony Club. With the support of The Pony Club Office, the committee is responsible for organising The Pony Club Championships for their sport. They will also maintain a separate Sport Rule Book which is published annually and they adjudicate on any matters requiring resolution within their sport. These Sport Rule Books form part of the Rules of The Pony Club.

Each Committee shall meet each year to consider whether any changes are required to the rules of their sport.

4.35 With the approval of the Management Committee, a newly appointed or re-appointed Sport Chairman may ask up to 50% of the Sport Committee to resign.

Training Committee

4.36 The Training Committee has responsibility for advising the Management Committee on:

- The training of Pony Club coaches;
- The training of Pony Club Members;
- All elements of horsemanship and horsemastership within competitions;
- The commissioning of coaching and training publications;
- All aspects of the A, AH and B Tests including the administration of tests;
- The appointments and removal of assessors to and from the Panel of Assessors for 'A' and 'AH' Tests.

4.37 The Training Committee shall meet annually to recommend any changes required to the syllabus of each Test, or to the fees charged for 'B' test and above.

Centre Membership Committee

4.38 The Centre Membership Committee has responsibility for advising the Management Committee on:

- The administration of the Centre Membership Scheme and all matters affecting the interests of Centre Members
- The criteria to be met and the standards required of Pony Club Centres to join the Centre Membership Scheme
- The approval for individual Riding Centres to join the Centre Membership Scheme.

4.39 To assist in carrying out this responsibility, the Committee will appoint Area Centre Coordinators to assess the suitability of Riding Centres.

Health and Safety and Safeguarding Advisory Committee

4.40 The Health and Safety and Safeguarding Advisory Committee will meet as required and will have responsibility for reviewing and advising the Trustees on:

- The Health and Safety Policy of The Pony Club
- The Pony Club Safeguarding Policy
- All matters concerning compliance with the safer recruitment requirements including disclosure checks and safeguarding training.

Rules and Compliance Committee

4.41 The Committee will be responsible for maintaining the Rules of The Pony Club and recommending changes to the Trustees as they may be required. The Committee will scrutinise the various rule books to ensure consistency and set codes of conduct and standards to apply throughout The Pony Club. All complaints and disputes will be dealt with by the Committee.

4.42 The Committee will elect a Chairman from amongst its number. The Branch Operations Directors will be members of the Committee. Two Area Representatives will also be members and the Committee will have power to co-opt additional members from time to time. It is recommended that one member of the Committee should have legal experience.

Volunteers and Officials Committee

4.43 The Committee will be responsible for the recruitment of volunteers to The Pony Club and for determining and maintaining the processes by which they are elected and for the appointment of Pony Club Ambassadors. The committee will also approve and/or ratify new District Commissioners.

4.44 The Committee will ensure that suitable training and development is provided for volunteers and that they are duly rewarded and recognised. The Committee will consult with volunteers as it sees fit.

4.45 The Committee will elect a Chairman from amongst its number. Membership of the Committee will comprise of persons appointed by the Company Members in general meeting but must include at least two Trustees and two Area Representatives. The Chairman of The Pony Club shall be ex officio a member of the Committee and may attend at his discretion. The Committee will have power to co-opt additional members from time to time.

Treasurer of The Pony Club

4.46 The Treasurer of the Pony Club shall be appointed by the Trustees and will hold office for a period of three years. Subject to Rule 3, a retiring Treasurer will be eligible for re-appointment for a further term of 3 years. The Treasurer, with the support of the Finance Manager, will be responsible for all financial matters affecting The Pony Club.

4.47 Not later than the end of October each year, the Treasurer of The Pony Club will submit to the Management Committee a draft budget for the following Pony Club Year, together with recommendations on annual subscriptions and capitation fees for that year. The Management Committee will then forward to the Trustees its recommendations as to the budget for the following Pony Club Year for approval (with or without modifications) by the Trustees.

4.48 At each Meeting of the Trustees, the Treasurer and/or the Finance Manager will give a financial report, during which they will comment on any material variations from the approved budget.

Chief Executive

4.49 The Chief Executive will be an employee of The Pony Club, responsible for administering the activities of The Pony Club and the Office within the policies and procedures established by the Trustees and in accordance with statutory requirements and the approved budget. He will report to the Chairman of The Pony Club and, through him, to the Trustees. He will attend all meetings of the Trustees, and all general meetings and such committee meetings as he may choose. He will have the right to speak at each such meeting but shall not have a vote, except on the Management Committee.

4.50 The Chief Executive may appoint or dismiss staff (other than members of the Senior Management Team) with the agreement of the Chairman of The Pony Club.

4.51 In the event of a vacancy for the position of Chief Executive or any other member of the Senior Management Team, the Trustees will establish a Recruitment sub-committee to recruit a new Chief Executive or member of the Senior Management Team as the case may be. This sub-committee will consist of no more than six members, to include the Chairman of The Pony Club (who will act as Chairman of the sub-committee) and the Treasurer of The Pony Club. The other members of the sub-committee will be drawn from the Trustees. The sub-committee will decide upon the selection policy and methods and will have absolute and irrevocable authority, on behalf of The Pony Club, to make an offer of employment to the candidate that it chooses. In the event of equality of votes, the Chairman of The Pony Club will have the casting vote.

The Handbook

4.52 The Pony Club Handbook will be published annually. It will include these Rules (but not the Sport Rules); annual subscriptions and test fees; names of the Trustees, the committees established under this Rule 4, Branch officials, Area Centre Coordinators and Centre Proprietors; details of Insurance cover and information on Pony Club merchandise. The Handbook may be published in electronic form.

Bankruptcy

4.53 Any Trustee, Company Member or District Commissioner, who becomes bankrupt or makes a composition with his creditors, shall be disqualified from office and his appointment shall be terminated immediately. No person who is an undischarged bankrupt may be appointed to any of these offices. This Rule shall also apply to any officer or member of a Branch Committee who has any responsibility for the financial affairs of the Branch.

5. CONFLICT OF INTEREST

5.1 At all levels of The Pony Club, from the Trustees to Branch Sub-Committees, avoidance of any potential conflict of interes must be strictly observed. Whenever an individual has a personal interest in a matte to be discussed at a meeting of a committe of which he is a member, he must: -

a. Declare his interest before discussion begins.
b. Be absent from the meeting for that item, unless expressly invited to remain provide information.
c. Not be counted in the quorum for that part of the meeting.
d. Be absent during the vote and have no vote on the matter.

5.2 Normally, a person who is an Equestrian Professional will not be eligible for appointment as an Area Representative or as a member of any committee or sub-committee established under these Rules (except for membership of the Centre Membership Committee or the Training Committee). The Management Committee however, at its discretion, may decide to approve the appointment of an Equestrian Professional and may attach to the approval such conditions as the Management Committee in its absolute discretion conside appropriate. In such a case, the person must submit a written declaration that he has read and understood the Conflict of Interest Policy of The Pony Club, as defined in this Rule, and that he will adhere to it. Equestriar Professionals who are members of any committee (including the Centre Membersh Committee and the Training Committee) or the Management Committee must also submit such a declaration. This Rule shall no be applied retrospectively.

5.3 A person empowered to take decisions on behalf of The Pony Club must ensure that those decisions are made in the best interest of The Pony Club.

6. MINUTES

6.1 All meetings of the Trustees, the Finance Committee, the Management Committee, the Health and Safety and Safeguarding Advisory Committee and the committees established under these Rules must be minuted and, subject to rule 6.2, copies of the minutes will be distributed to all members of these bodies, whether they were present at the meeting or not. Copies of the minutes will also be distributed as follows: -

- The Finance Committee – to the Trustees, and Management Committee
- The Management Committee – to the Trustees, the Rules and Compliance Committee, the Finance Committee, Area Representatives and Branch Operations Directors
- The Health and Safety and Safeguarding Advisory Committee – to the Trustees, Area Representatives and Branch Operations Directors
- The committees established under these Rules – to the Management Committee, the Rules and Compliance Committee, Area Representatives and Branch Operations Directors

6.2 Where a matter which is confidential (by reason of data protection legislation or otherwise) or the disclosure of which could prejudice the financial interests of The Pony Club is included in the minutes of any meeting, a summarised version of the minute omitting such details as will remove that prejudice, may be distributed to the relevant persons provided that the minute includes an indication of the general nature of the matter discussed.

7. MEMBERSHIP

Eligibility

7.1 Membership is available to anyone until the end of the Membership Subscription year in which he becomes 25 years old. Membership may be as a Branch or as a Centre Member. Membership as a Branch Member may be as a Riding Member or Non-Riding Member.

7.2 Where membership is of a Branch, a Member cannot join more than one Branch at one time. Usually, Branches accept any application for membership from people resident within their Branch District. Applications to join other Branches must be agreed with the Area Representative.

7.3 Centre Membership is intended for anyone who does not have their own pony, (either owned, hired or on loan), who rides at a Pony Club Linked Riding Centre.

7.4 Centre Plus Membership is for anyone who rides at a Centre and also has regular access to a horse/pony (whether owned by them, leased to them or loaned to them) to ride outside of Centre organised activities.

Termination of Membership

7.5 If the Renewal Subscription of any Branch Member has not been paid by the end of his Membership Subscription Year, membership is terminated from that date. As insurance cover will also cease at the same time, it is essential that a person whose membership has terminated must not be permitted to take part in any Branch or Centre activities, except those that are open to non-Members, until such time as he renews his membership of The Pony Club.

7.6 A District Commissioner may at any time recommend to his Branch Committee that they end the membership of any Branch Member who, in the opinion of the District Commissioner, shows insufficient interest in their Branch. The District Commissioner may, at his own discretion, make a Branch rule that Members, to remain in membership of the Branch, participate in Branch activities, be selected to represent the Branch in any competition or be nominated to represent The Pony Club, **should demonstrate an interest in and a commitment to the Branch. This may include a requirement that the member attends** a certain number or percentage of the working rallies of the Branch in a calendar year unless prevented from doing so by illness, absence from home or any other reason which in the opinion of the District Commissioner justifies absence. **The Rules and Compliance Committee may issue guidance to Branch Committees about the extent and type of rule that may be made under this provision.**

7.7 If it is proposed to end the membership of any Member, notice will be given to the Member after consultation with their Area Representative who then may make appropriate representations. The Chairman of The Pony Club or the Chief Executive may suspend any Member whose conduct is under investigation.

7.8 The Rules and Compliance Committee may expel or temporarily exclude from the benefits of membership, any Member whose conduct is such, in its opinion, as to be injurious or detrimental to the character or reputation of The Pony Club or of any of its Branches or Centres or to the interests of The Pony Club or its Members or whose conduct shall in the opinion of the Committee, make a Member unfit or unsuitable to continue as a Member. In the case of a Branch Member, the request for such an expulsion will be initiated by the decision of a Branch Committee to recommend to their Area Representative the expulsion of the Member. The Area Representative will then present the case to the Rules and Compliance Committee. In the case of a Centre Member, or Centre Plus Member an Area Centre Coordinator will recommend the expulsion to the Chairman of the Centre Membership Committee, who will present the case to the Rules and Compliance Committee.

7.9 Before the Rules and Compliance Committee expels or temporarily excludes a Member, he will be given reasonable notice of relevant meetings, and the full opportunity to defend himself, and to justify or explain his conduct. This will include making representations by way of defence, justification and explanation on behalf of the Member by his parents. If the Rules and Compliance Committee is of the opinion that the Member has been guilty of the alleged conduct and that the Member or parents of such Member has or have failed to justify or explain it satisfactorily, the Rules and Compliance Committee shall decide either to expel or temporarily exclude the Member from The Pony Club.

7.10 The Rules and Compliance Committee may also terminate the membership of a Member on medical grounds, if it considers that the continuation of membership would be dangerous or detrimental to either the Member himself or to others. In reaching its decision, the Rules and Compliance Committee shall take into account such medical reports that may be available to it, but the absence of any medical reports shall not preclude the Rules and Compliance Committee from terminating the Member's membership.

7.11 Before the Rules and Compliance Committee terminates membership on medical grounds, the Member will be given reasonable notice of relevant meetings, and full opportunity to justify his continued membership. This will include making representations by way of justification and explanation on behalf of the Member by his parents and/or by appropriate medical professionals.

7.12 If a majority of the Rules and Compliance Committee present at the inquiry is of the opinion that the Member's medical condition satisfies the criteria specified above, then his membership will be terminated.

7.13 The Area Representative or the Chairman of the Centre Membership Committee (as appropriate) has the authority to suspend the Member from membership pending the Rules and Compliance Committee inquiry.

7.14 On the termination of membership for medical reasons, the Member will be entitled to a pro-rata refund of the subscription and/or fees paid for the current year.

7.15 A District Commissioner may refuse to accept an application for membership. With the approval of the Area Representative, he may also refuse to renew the membership of a Member. Reasons for such action would normally be given.

7.16 If a District Commissioner refuses to renew a Member's membership, that person may apply to join another Branch. In such a case Rule 8 (Transfers) will apply, save for the following: -

- The Transfer Form does not need the approval of the refusing District Commissioner.
- The 14 months rule will apply to the Member refused. However, any other children of the family may elect to transfer to the same Branch, without the imposition of the 14 months rule.

7.17 On the ending of membership, whether because of age, non-payment of subscription, resignation, expulsion or any other reason whatever, the Member will forfeit all the privileges of membership and all rights against The Pony Club. Subscriptions will not, except as provided above, be returnable and the Member will still be liable for all annual subscriptions that had become due and remained unpaid at the date of ending of his membership.

Parents and Supporters

7.18 The Pony Club publishes on its website information on the role of parents and expects parents and those with parental responsibility to comply with the guidance set out there.

7.19 Where the behaviour of a parent or supporter is considered to be detrimental to the conduct of Branch activities it may be necessary first to give a warning and ultimately (although The Pony Club may dispense with a warning in exceptional cases) to ban them from attending Pony Club activities. The parent or supporter should be informed of any such decision by means of a letter from the District Commissioner which should indicate the reasons for the decision and indicate that the parent or supporter can appeal against the warning to the Rules and Compliance Committee. Such appeal must be made within three weeks of receipt of the letter. They should also be informed that the Member with whom they are associated is still welcome at Pony Club activities and that the District Commissioner will indicate on entry forms to competitions run by other Branches that the parent has been banned from attending Pony Club activities.

8. BRANCH MEMBERSHIP AND TRANSFERS

Subscription

8.1 The Trustees will set the rate for the Annual Subscription and will publish this in the Handbook or on the website. They will also determine the capitation fee, which is that part of the Annual Subscription retained by the Pony Club Office or (as the case may be) paid by Branches to The Pony Club Office. A new Branch is exempted from paying the capitation fee in The Pony Club Year in which it is formed.

8.2 The first annual subscription is due when first applying for membership. Membership runs for twelve months from the date the subscription is received. A renewal reminder will be sent to the Member one month before the end of his Membership Subscription Year. Email Renewal reminders will be sent to the Member in the month leading up to the end of the Membership Subscription Year.

8.3 Applications for membership or to renew membership may be made online through the approved Pony Club portal or on the official Branch Membership Application Form or the official Branch Membership Renewal Form issued by the Office. If Branches require additional information that is not included on these forms, this may be collected by means of a locally produced supplementary form, but this must be in addition to the official forms, not replacing them.

8.4 For the purposes of this Rule, a renewing Member is one who renews his membership and who has at any time in the past been a Member of any Branch of the Pony Club. His previous branch may not necessarily be the Branch that he is now applying to join.

8.5 A new Member is somebody who joins a Branch for the first time and has never previously been a Branch Member (although he could have been a Centre Member).

8.6 Family Membership is available up to a maximum of 5 children of the family (as defined in rule 2). Children to be covered by family membership must all live at the same permanent address and must be Members of the same Branch.

8.7 Where there is/are already one or two child/children in a family who are Members, and additional Children of the Family join or renew their membership, thereby meaning they would qualify for Family Membership, a new Family Membership for all the Children of the Family will be deemed to have commenced on the date of joining of the additional child(ren) which will terminate on the day before the anniversary of this date. The parent will then be liable to pay the then current Family Membership Fee less an amount equal to the proportion of the membership fees paid in respect of those children who were already members that is equivalent to the unexpired portion of each such member's Membership Subscription Year.

Visiting Members

8.8 All Members will be welcomed as occasional visitors at working rallies or other activities of a Branch/Centre other than their own Branch/Centre, provided that the agreement of both District Commissioners/ Centre Proprietors is obtained. A Visiting Member cannot represent the Branch/ Centre that he is visiting in any Pony Club competitions. He may not take tests (other than Achievement Badges) at that other Branch/Centre without the permission of his own District Commissioner/Centre Proprietor

Transfers

8.9 Transfers are not encouraged, as The Pony Club believes they are not in the best interests of The Pony Club as a whole but any member wishing to transfer should submit a Transfer Request via the Pony Club Website.

8.10 (a) Where the transfer involves a member moving from

- **one Branch to another Branch**
- **a Branch to Centre Plus Membership**
- **Centre Plus membership to a Branch**

notice of the Transfer Request will be given to the Area Representative(s) and District

Commissioner(s)/Centre Proprietor of both the current and proposed Branches/ Centre for their approval. If the transfer is approved by the Area Representative(s) and by the District Commissioner(s)/Centre Proprietor concerned it can go ahead. In all other cases the transfer will be processed by the Membership team in the Pony Club Office and be allowed without the need for further approval.

(b) If, within 21 days of receiving notice of the proposed transfer, any of the Area Representatives or District Commissioner(s)/Centre Proprietor notified under this rule has not notified the Membership Team that he/she disagrees with the transfer or that he requires further time to consider the proposed transfer, it shall be deemed to have been approved.

(c) If the proposed transfer is not approved by any relevant person, an appeal may be made by or on behalf of the Member to the Rules and Compliance Committee, which will have the absolute discretion and authority to approve or reject any transfer. The Committee may give reasons for its decision but is not obliged to do so.

(d) In reaching a decision the Rules and Compliance Committee will determine what, if any, representations of interested parties (if any) are appropriate and will give reasonable and adequate notice of any meetings. The decision of the Rules and Compliance Committee shall be final.

8.11 Subject to Rules 8.12 and 8.13, a Member who transfers in any of the circumstances listed in Rule 8.10 (a) may not compete in any Championship qualifying competition as a Team Member for fourteen calendar months from the date of transfer. Such a Member may, however, compete as an individual in any such competitions. Any transferred Member ineligible under this rule to compete at an Area Team qualifying competition shall not be eligible to compete at the later stages of the competition in the Pony Club Year that the restriction expires. A Member may appeal to the Rules and Compliance Committee against the imposition of this rule.

8.12 The restriction on competing as a Team member imposed by virtue of rule 8.11 shall not apply

(a) if the Transfer Request is made within 12 months of first joining The Pony Club.

(b) if the Transfer Request is as a result of a permanent change of residence into another Branch/Centre's district, provided the Transfer Request is made within 12 calendar months of the permanent change of residence.

(c) to any sport in which during the 24 months prior to the date of Transfer Request, the Member has not competed in any Pony Club competition at any level in that sport for his previous Branch/Centre.

(d) if the Transfer Request is made because the Branch/Centre to which the Member currently belongs does not offer the opportunity to take part in Mounted Games, Polo or Polocrosse at any level, be it rallies, friendly competitions or Area Competitions, in which case the fourteen months restriction will not apply to that sport, but it will apply to any other sports in which he could have taken part.

(e) to the Regional Championships, the Quiz, and the Horse and Pony Care competitions.

8.13 For the avoidance of doubt, a Renewing Member who applies to join a different Branch/Centre is subject to the transfer provisions as set out above and a

Transfer Request must be submitted.

8.14 In the year of transfer, if the transfer is from one Branch to another, no part of the Annual Subscription of a Member will be payable to the "receiving" Branch unless the Annual Subscription is paid to the "receiving" Branch after the transfer.

Branches outside the UK

8.15 The Rules of The Pony Club apply only to Great Britain and Northern Ireland.

8.16 Any Club situated outside Great Britain and Northern Ireland and having objects similar to those of The Pony Club may, with its approval, be affiliated to The Pony Club and when and so long as it is affiliated it must be known by a name indicating that it is a Branch of The Pony Club.

8.17 Any affiliated Club, Advisory Board or Committee will make any rules for its constitution and organisation as it shall think fit, but these rules must first be sent to and approved by The Pony Club who may require any amendments and additions and deletions as it thinks proper.

8.18 In any event approval will be withheld unless the rules incorporate the objects and spirit of the Rules of The Pony Club.

8.19 A Member of an affiliated Overseas Branch can transfer to a UK Branch and become a full Member. The same conditions will apply as for British Members (see Transfer rule).

8.20 Affiliated Clubs will contribute an affiliation fee to The Pony Club, which will be set by the Trustees.

8.21 Any approval by The Pony Club given to Affiliated Clubs may at any time be withdrawn when all privileges will be terminated. Adequate notice will be given, along with reasons for withdrawal, in reasonable time.

The Pony Club from time to time may also vary the conditions of membership and the Rules of Affiliated Clubs, upon reasonable notice.

9. AREA AND BRANCH ORGANISATION

Areas and Branches

9.1 The Pony Club's administration in the UK is divided into Areas, which are defined by the Area Representatives Committee. Each Area will be headed by an Area Representative. Areas consist of a number of Branches and the Area Representative will agree the geographical boundary of each Branch. The creation of a new Branch, or the amalgamation of existing Branches, must have the prior agreement of the Area Representative. If a Branch cannot agree its boundaries with the Area Representative, it will have the right of appeal to the Management Committee. It is permissible for Branches to have overlapping boundaries.

9.2 Branches must follow the purposes of The Pony Club, as stated in Rule 1.1 and are governed by the Rules of The Pony Club.

9.3 The Rules and Compliance Committee shall have the power to suspend or expel a Branch or an officer or committee member of that Branch, if it believes there to be a breach of this requirement. Similar action may be taken if it believes that The Pony Club is being brought into disrepute.

9.4 Before the Rules and Compliance Committee suspends or expels a Branch, the District Commissioner and Branch Secretary will be given reasonable notice of relevant meetings, and full opportunity to defend the Branch and to justify or explain its conduct.

9.5 This will include making representation by way of defence, justification and explanation on its behalf. If the majority of the Rules and Compliance Committee present is of the opinion that the Branch is in breach of its obligations and that its representatives have failed to justify or explain it satisfactorily, the Rules and Compliance Committee shall decide either to suspend or to expel the Branch.

9.6 In the case of the proposed suspension or expulsion of an officer or committee member, they shall be entitled to similar notice periods and entitlement to defence.

Area Representatives

9.7 The District Commissioners in each Area will elect, from amongst themselves or from outside, an Area Representative. On a vacancy, or in June of the third year of an Area Representative's term, the Pony Club Office will ask the District Commissioners in that Area to nominate their choice, having confirmed that the person concerned is willing to stand. The Pony Club Office will then organise a vote. District Commissioners can nominate themselves.

9.8 The appointment of a person as Area Representative will be subject to confirmation by the Management Committee. They will hold office for three years from 1st January after the date of their election and will be eligible for re-election. They will represent their Area on the Area Representatives Committee and will offer help and advice to District Commissioners and/ or their committees on the organisation and administration of the individual Branches in their Area.

9.9 The responsibilities of Area Representatives include:

- To ensure that their Branches are aware of and adhere to the Health and Safety and Safeguarding Policies, and other statutory obligations.
- To hold at least two Area Meetings per year.
- To co-ordinate with Branches and Centres in the Area the dates of competitions, coaching courses and training days and to arrange organisers, dates and venues for Area competitions.
- To find out the views and wishes of their Branches and represent those views when required to the Office.
- To liaise with appropriate committees and or members of staff.
- To pass to the Pony Club Office anything in the Area that requires its attention.
- To advise the Volunteers and Officials Committee of the suitability of new District Commissioners elected by Branches in their Area and of new Branches proposed in their Area.
- To handle complaints.
- To give, when appropriate, general advice, help and support to District Commissioners and Centre Proprietors and if necessary, to exercise supervision on;
    - The appointment of new District Commissioners
    - Branch problems
    - Branch programmes
    - Health and Safety and Safeguarding
- To approve transfers between Branches
- To advise on the accreditation of Coaches and Nominees for the Visiting Coaches Panel and National Assessors' Panel.
- To organise or delegate the responsibility of organising Area Training courses for Coaches, Assessors for 'AH' and 'B' Test levels, and candidates for the higher Tests as required by their Branches/Centres.
- To approve 'A' Test nominations.
- To have an up-to-date panel of Assessors for 'B' Tests and send it to The Pony Club Office each year.
- To organise, or delegate the responsibility for appointing, suitable 'B' Test Assessors to attend a study day to make sure there is a level standard of examining for the

Test in the Area. Assessors should attend at least one study day every two years to remain on the Area Panel.

- To keep a record of passes at AH, B+ and all levels of 'B' Tests.
- To advise the Pony Club Office of any views from their Area on new riding establishments applying to become a Pony Club Linked Riding Centre.
- To assist Centre Proprietors to find Assessors for Pony Club Tests up to and including 'C+' Standard.
- To let the Pony Club Office know of any suitable Members from their Area for overseas visits and other events.
- To inform the Pony Club Office of any suitable students for any nationally organised course, such as the 'A' Test Coaching Camp
- To ensure financial records are kept for any accounts held by the Area such that, Annual Accounts for Areas (including those for Area Sports) are sent to The Pony Club Office on the form provided. A completed Area Annual Financial Return submission will encompass:
    - Fully completed, balanced return signed by the AR or the delegated officer: and
    - Bank statements and building society pass books showing the balance as at 31st December.

9.10 If an Area Representative loses the confidence of his District Commissioners, and he is unwilling to resign, then this should be reported to the Rules and Compliance Committee in writing and signed by a majority of the District Commissioners in the Area.

9.11 The Rules and Compliance Committee will appoint a person to investigate fully and, if necessary, to report. The Rules and Compliance Committee in its absolute discretion may end the appointment of an Area Representative at any time upon giving written notice to the individual.

9.12 The Rules and Compliance Committee will normally seek representations from the individual concerned and will give reasons for its decision. However, in certain circumstances (which it may in its absolute discretion determine) it may decide not to give reasons.

9.13 Area Representatives will be reimbursed expenses incurred by them in accordance with the Pony Club Expenses Policy.

Area Meetings

9.14 At least twice per year, Area Representatives will hold meetings with the District Commissioners (or their representatives) in their Area. If so wished, these may be open meetings. The purpose of these meetings shall be to provide a forum for debating areas of concern. Area Representatives should obtain the views of their District Commissioners on these matters whilst recognising the independence of individual Branches to conduct their own activities, subject to the ultimate authority of the Management Committee. One of the meetings shall be held in the autumn, prior to the Annual General Meeting.

District Commissioners

9.15 Each Branch will be managed by a Branch Committee **chaired by** its District Commissioner. The first District Commissioner of a **new** Branch will be appointed for three years by the Volunteers and Officials Committee on the recommendation of the Area Representative. **Thereafter the District Commissioner will be appointed by the Branch Committee.**

9.16 If a District Commissioner is appointed before 1st July in the calendar year, his term will end at the third 31st December after the date of his

appointment. If he is appointed after 30th June, his term will end at the fourth 31st December after the date of his appointment. A District Commissioner does not need to be a member of the Branch Committee before election.

9.17 When the term of office of a District Commissioner is due to expire, the Branch Committee will meet to arrange to elect his successor, although the retiring District Commissioner may offer himself for re-election. If he is offering himself for re-election, the retiring District Commissioner cannot vote in this election, and must retire from the meeting whilst the election and votes take place.

9.18 If the retiring District Commissioner is not standing for re-election then he does not have to retire from the meeting and will continue to act as Chairman of the Branch Committee until the end of his period of office. If the District Commissioner is not present and the Branch has appointed an Assistant District Commissioner who is present, he will chair the meeting, otherwise the members of the Branch Committee present at that meeting will appoint a person present to act as Chairman for the election. In the event of an equality of votes, the person chairing the meeting will have a casting vote.

9.19 In the event of there being more than one candidate for District Commissioner, the election will be by secret ballot and it will be the responsibility of the Branch Secretary to provide a sufficient number of ballot papers for each Committee member present to vote. All candidates nominated for District Commissioner will retire from the meeting when the ballot is taking place and will not return until all the votes have been counted and the result given to the person chairing the meeting. Candidates will not have a vote.

9.20 A newly elected District Commissioner will take office on the next 1st January, unless the position of District Commissioner is vacant, in which case he will take office immediately.

9.21 A retiring District Commissioner may not serve as a Committee member of the same Branch for a period of one year from the date of his retirement except in exceptional circumstances and with the approval of the Rules and Compliance Committee.

9.22 The appointment of the District Commissioner elected will be subject to the approval of the Volunteers and Officials Committee which will take the opinion of the Area Representative into account. If the new District Commissioner has not yet attended a **'Branch Officials'** training day, his appointment will be conditional, and will not be confirmed until he has attended such a day. If the new District Commissioner has not attended a District Commissioners' Training Day within 12 months of receiving conditional approval, his Area Representative must either revoke his appointment or grant him an extension of time. The maximum extension allowed is one further period of 12 months. Until the approval and training process is completed, a new District Commissioner will run the Branch in an acting capacity.

9.23 In exceptional circumstances, and at the discretion of the Volunteers and Officials Committee, two Joint District Commissioners of a Branch may be appointed. However, in this event, one of the District Commissioners must agree to accept the ultimate responsibility for carrying out the duties and responsibilities of a District Commissioner, as detailed in Rule 9.28 below.

9.24 Normally a person who is an

Equestrian Professional will not be eligible for appointment as a District Commissioner. The Volunteers and Officials Committee however, at its absolute discretion, may decide to approve the appointment of an Equestrian Professional as a District Commissioner and may attach to the approval such conditions as the Volunteers and Officials Committee in its absolute discretion considers appropriate. In such a case, the person must submit a written declaration that he has read and understood the Conflict of Interest Policy of The Pony Club, as defined in Rule 5 and that he will adhere to it.

9.25 If any person ceases to be a District Commissioner for any reason, or if a District Commissioner elected by a Branch Committee is not approved by the Volunteers and Officials Committee, the Branch Committee will immediately hold a committee meeting and will elect a District Commissioner to take the place of the existing one. The District Commissioner thus elected will hold office for three years. Such an election will be subject to the approval of the Volunteers and Officials Committee and the training process as detailed above.

9.26 The Volunteers and Officials Committee generally will, but is not required to, give reasons for not giving its approval of the appointment of a District Commissioner elected by a Branch Committee. It may allow representations from the candidate.

9.27 A District Commissioner is not allowed to make cash or other financial contribution towards the expenses of his Branch. This does not preclude a District Commissioner from waiving repayment of his travelling or out of pocket expenses, if he so wishes.

9.28 The responsibilities of District Commissioners are to ensure that:

- The Branch complies fully with the Health and Safety and Safeguarding Policies, and other statutory obligations.
- They are familiar with The Pony Club's Health and Safety Rule Book and Safeguarding Policy and that a copy is given to every Camp Organiser.
- Camps, Rallies, lectures and other events are organised for the Branch Members.
- The membership database for the branc reflects the members of the branch and any anomalies are reported to The Pony Club Office as soon as noted.
- Joining fees and Annual Subscriptions ar collected.
- All returns and money required by the Rules are sent to the Pony Club Office according to the established timetable.
- The names of Coaches used by the Branch, and their qualifications, are entered on the Coach Directory section o the Pony Club database.
- Minutes are taken of all Branch Committee Meetings and Annual Meetings and are kept in a Minute Book.
- Simple financial accounts for the Branch are kept and arrangements made for the inspection of them if required by the Trustees. A financial statement should be produced at each meeting of the Branch Committee.
- Accounts are audited yearly by an appropriate person or reviewed by a member of the Branch Committee who i either case is not related in any way to the Treasurer and does not live at the same address as the Treasurer.
- Annual accounts are sent to The Pony Club Office on the form provided. The accounts of all Sub-Committees, Parents' Associations or Support Groups must be included in the Branch Return.
- A register is kept of all the fixed assets (land, buildings, vehicles, caravans, trailers jumps, trophies and other equipment belonging to the Branch, whether or not the Branch capitalises fixed assets in its accounts. Items costing or valued

(whichever is the greater) less than £100 need not be entered on the register Property comprising a set should be priced as a set, not as individual items. This register must be physically checked at least once every year.

- The Branch Committee is made aware of all, important information from the Pony Club Office.
- Any other tasks and responsibilities that are given by the Management Committee are carried out.

The DC will usually delegate the following duties and responsibilities to the Branch Treasurer, but the DC is ultimately responsible to ensure :

- Appropriate financial records are kept as detailed in section 21.18.
- The Branch holds a bank account with at least 2 signatories
- Simple financial accounts for the Branch are kept and arrangements made for the inspection of them if required by the Trustees.
- A financial statement is produced at each meeting of the Branch Committee.
- Accounts are audited yearly by an appropriate person or reviewed by a member of the Branch Committee who in either case is not related in any way to the Treasurer and does not live at the same address as the Treasurer.
- Branch Financial Returns which include annual accounts are sent to The Pony Club Office on the form provided. The accounts of all Sub-Committees, Parents' Associations or Support Groups must be included in the Branch Return.
- A register is kept of all the fixed assets (land, buildings, vehicles, caravans, trailers, jumps, trophies and other equipment belonging to the Branch, whether or not the Branch capitalises fixed assets in its accounts. Items costing or valued (whichever is the greater) less than £250 need not be entered on the register. Property comprising a set should be priced as a set, not as individual items. This register must be physically checked at least once every year.
- Cash transactions are kept to a minimum as per Section 21.25 (new section).
- Payments made to coaches and other camp helpers are done in line with rule 12.3.
- Expense payments made are in accordance with rules 12.4 and 12.5.

Branch Committee and Committee Members

9.29 The Branch Committee will consist of no fewer than five people including the District Commissioner and will be responsible for appointing the following Officers of the Branch: Branch Secretary, Branch Treasurer, Health and Safety Officer, and Branch Safeguarding Officer who will be members of the Branch Committee. A person, including the District Commissioner, may hold more than one appointment, except that the Treasurer may not be the District Commissioner, nor may he be anybody residing at the same address as the District Commissioner. Additionally, the Committee may appoint an Assistant District Commissioner. A Branch Committee can at any time increase or reduce its number provided that it shall not be fewer than five. To do this or to fill casual vacancies, the Committee can at any time elect new members to join the Committee.

9.30 No person may be appointed or re-appointed to the Committee of more than one Branch.

9.31 The appointment of all members of the Branch Committee will be for a fixed term and must be recorded in the minutes of the Committee. If appointed before 1st

July in the calendar year, their term will end at the third 31st December after the date of their appointment. If appointed after 30th June, their term will end at the fourth 31st December after the date of their appointment. In either case a member of the Branch Committee may offer himself for re-appointment.

9.32 The Branch Committee will hold a meeting during the final three months of the year to elect persons to fill any vacancy arising at the end of that year by virtue of the expiry of the term of office of any member of the Branch Committee, although the retiring member may offer himself for re-election. If he is offering himself for re-election, the retiring member may not vote in this election, and must retire from the meeting whilst the election and votes take place.

9.33 If requested to do so by the Area Representative, a Branch shall supply to the Area Representative a list of all members of the Branch Committee and the date on which they were each appointed and if it appears to the Area Representative that a Branch has failed to hold elections in accordance with Rule 9.17 or 9.32, the Area Representative shall have power to suspend any member of the Branch Committee (including for the avoidance of doubt the District Commissioner) until such time as the Area Representative is satisfied that an election to fill the post(s) has been conducted by the Branch in accordance with these rules.

9.34 In exceptional circumstances, after consultation with and with the approval of the Area Representative, a newly appointed District Commissioner who has attended a Branch officials training day, may ask up to 50% of the Branch Committee to resign.

9.35 The District Commissioner will be the Chairman of the Branch Committee. However, if he is unable to be present at a Committee meeting, the Assistant District Commissioner (if appointed) will be the Chairman. Otherwise the other members present shall choose one of their number to chair the meeting. The Branch Committee of each Branch will meet at least four times each year. A quorum will consist of not less than three members. Questions at any meeting will be decided by a majority vote. In the case of an equality of votes the Chairman will have a casting vote. If a member of the Branch Committee cannot attend a meeting, they cannot nominate an alternate person to attend on their behalf.

9.36 The Branch Treasurer must present an Income and Expenditure Account and a Balance Sheet for the previous Pony Club Year, for approval by the Branch Committee. This should be done no later than the first Branch Committee meeting after the end of the relevant Pony Club Year.

9.37 The accounting records of the Branch (including, but not limited to, ledgers, bank statements, invoices, cheque books and counterfoils, paying in books and counterfoils, pass books and computerised records) are the property of the Branch. Should the accounts be kept on a computer, then the rights to use any proprietary software (including serial numbers and activation codes) must be owned by the Branch. Accounting records kept in a computer must be securely backed up at regular intervals, at least monthly. If the computer system is password protected, the password must be known by another member of the Branch Committee as well as the Treasurer.

NB Regulation of charities has become increasingly strict, particularly in regard to the management of finances. A pamphlet "Guidelines for Branch Treasurers" is issued to all Branch Treasurers and District

Commissioners and is also available on the website. This gives advice on the duties and responsibilities of Branch Treasurers.

9.38 Should it appear that a Branch Treasurer or any other person carrying out the functions of a Branch Treasurer, or any other person performing financial functions for the Branch (such as cheque signing or handling cash), is not providing the required level of financial stewardship, the Rules and Compliance Committee may suspend them from office, and order that all of the Branch's financial records and documents should be surrendered to a named person. In the period between Rules and Compliance Committee meetings, the Treasurer of The Pony Club may initiate the suspension and if the official concerned is the Branch Treasurer he will, if required to do so by the Area Representative, surrender all of the Branch's financial records and documents to a named person pending the outcome of the matter

9.39 The Rules and Compliance Committee shall order an investigation into the complaint against the suspended person. Depending on the outcome of this investigation, he may either be reinstated or removed from office. In the latter case, he shall have the right to appeal to the Appeal Committee, the decision of which shall be final.

9.40 If a Branch Committee passes a Vote of No Confidence in the District Commissioner or any other member of the Branch Committee, and he is unwilling to resign, then this will be reported to the Area Representative. The Area Representative will arrange for an investigation into the matter to be undertaken either personally or by some other person appointed by him and for the result of the investigation to be reported to the Rules and Compliance Committee for a decision as to whether to terminate the appointment of the individual concerned. Pending a decision by the Rules and Compliance Committee the District Commissioner or Branch Committee member concerned shall be suspended from acting in that capacity.

9.41 The Area Representative or the Rules and Compliance Committee may also initiate an investigation into the conduct of a District Commissioner or other Branch Committee member. The Committee may deem it appropriate that a person other than the Branch's Area Representative should carry out any investigation. The Rules and Compliance Committee, in its absolute discretion, may end the appointment of a District Commissioner or Branch Committee member at any time upon giving written notice, both to the individual and to the Branch Secretary. The Committee would normally seek representations from the individual concerned and would give reasons for its decision. However, in certain circumstances (which it may in its absolute discretion determine) it may decide not to give reasons.

9.42 A Branch Committee may create one or more sub-branches in outlying parts of the District covered by the Branch. These sub-branches will be managed by the Branch Committee who can appoint a sub-committee for that purpose. The District Commissioner and at least one other member of the Branch Committee will be members of any sub- committee or any Parents' Associations/ Support Groups, etc established.

9.43 The funds of any sub-branches, Parents' Associations, or any other Support Group and their use are under the control of the District Commissioner and the Branch Committee, and they may instruct that all or part of such funds shall be transferred to the Branch account.

Parents' Meeting

9.44 Each Branch must hold a Parents' Meeting annually, open to Parents and

Members. As a minimum, the Meeting must include a report from the District Commissioner on the activities of the past year, the presentation of a simple financial statement by the Treasurer, and questions and opinions from the floor. Other reports may be given as appropriate, and awards may be presented. This Meeting has no authority to impose decisions on the Branch Committee but the Branch Committee shall in making any decision have due regard to any views expressed at a Parents' Meeting.

Branch Presidents

9.45 A Branch Committee may have a Branch President, but a person shall not by virtue only of being the President become a member of the Branch Committee. Presidents shall serve for a three-year term, terminating at the third 31st December after the date of their appointment. They can be re- appointed by the invitation of the Branch Committee.

Amalgamation and closing of Branches

9.46 If the Management Committee, in its absolute discretion considers that a Branch has become so small as to be unable to provide an adequate quality or variety of activities to its Members or that the continued operation of the Branch will prejudice the effective, efficient and economic management of The Pony Club, the Management Committee may require the Branch to amalgamate with an adjoining Branch.

9.47 The Management Committee shall not exercise its power in Rule 9.46 to require a Branch to amalgamate with an adjoining Branch unless it has first given to the District Commissioner and Branch Secretary of both Branches, notice of its intention to do so. The notice may include details of any improvement(s) the Management Committee would consider a Branch needs to make to avoid the Management Committee taking such action and of any reasonable period within which such improvement(s) must be made. The District Commissioner and Branch Secretary will be given reasonable notice of relevant meetings, and full opportunity to present reasons why the Branch should not be amalgamated with an adjoining Branch.

9.48 If a Branch, for whatever reason, ceases to exist it is the duty of the District Commissioner, or if there is not a District Commissioner then of the Secretary of the Branch Committee, to send the following to The Pony Club Office: -

- All the funds of the Branch and of any sub branch(es) under the management of the Branch Committee.
- All the Branch membership records, including those of any sub-branch(es).
- All financial books and statements of the Branch and any sub-branch(es)
- The Minute Books of the Branch and of any sub-branch(es).
- All other significant documents held by the Branch and any sub-branch(es).
- An inventory of all equipment held and owned by the Branch and any sub-branch(es).

9.49 The Management Committee shall decide the disposition of Branch equipment and assets, although it may delegate this decision to the Area Representative.

9.50 The Branch Secretary must send a copy of the minutes of every meeting of the Branch Committee and any subcommittee thereof to the Area Representative.

10. BRANCH ACTIVITIES

Scope

10.1 Branches have the right to arrange their own programme of activities, subject only to compliance with these Rules and to any directions that may be given by the Area Representatives Committee or the Management Committee. A Branch Programme, listing forthcoming activities approved by the District Commissioner, should be given to all Members at regular intervals.

10.2 A Branch will not hold an activity in the District of any other Branch (unless it is in shared territory) except by invitation or permission of the other District Commissioner. This should not unreasonably be refused. This Rule shall not apply to commercial premises.

Welfare

10.3 At Pony Club Rallies and other mounted activities, the following are unacceptable: -

- ponies that are aged under four years.
- ponies that are infirm through old age;
- ponies that are ill, thin or lame;
- ponies that are a danger to their riders or to other Members or their ponies;
- mares that are heavy in-foal, mares in milk and mares with foal at foot;
- obese ponies.

10.4 Stallions can only be ridden at Pony Club events by Members if they obtain written permission from their District Commissioner and must wear identifying discs on their bridle in the interests of safety.

10.5 All ponies are expected to be properly groomed and well turned out, with correctly fitting tack.

10.6 If Branches incur expenses to pay for Coaches and/or facilities, it is permissible to charge Members a commensurate fee for attendance at an activity. Membership of The Pony Club does not confer any right to free rallies, although these may be given if funds permit.

Rallies / Coaching / Training Sessions

10.7 To be eligible to compete at Area Competitions and above, Members and their horse/pony must have actively taken part in a minimum of three Rallies/ Qualifying Coaching/Training Sessions since 1st July in the previous year. Individual sports may adopt more stringent requirements. Below this level, Branches/ Centres may adopt their own policy. For the purposes of this rule a Rally/Qualifying Coaching/Training Session is one which is organised by a Branch Committee , the Area Representative or by the Training Committee and must be a minimum of one hour in length. Each day of a camp shall be counted as a separate Rally/Coaching/ Training Session.

10.8 To count as a Rally/Qualifying Coaching/Training Session it must be open to all Members within the age range or ability level for which it is intended. It may be mounted or unmounted and must have been advertised at least seven days prior to the date of the event. Team practices do not count as Rally/Qualifying Coaching/ Training Sessions Nobody can organise a Branch Rally/Coaching/Training Session or coach at a Branch Coaching/Training Session unless authorised by the District Commissioner.

10.9 If , as a result of rule 10.7 a member would be ineligible to compete at any competition, an application may be submitted to the Rules and Compliance Committee to waive the rule in that Member's case.

Practices

10.10 Practices for the various sport competitions shall be announced in the Branch Programme, so that all eligible Members wishing to take part may do so. Any additional practices that are arranged within the period covered by the current Branch Programme, but after the Programme has been distributed, must have the approval of the District Commissioner.

Pony Club Camps

10.11 A Camp is an assembly of The Pony Club Members, together with ponies, held over a period of several days, usually during the summer holidays. It may be either residential or non-residential for both Members and ponies. The object of Camp is to provide an instructional holiday for Members and their ponies. Training should be given each day, but the holiday element must not be neglected and there should be a balanced mix of enjoyable activities and competitions. Not all of these activities and competitions need to be equestrian in nature. Camp is intended to be fun.

10.12 In view of the additional responsibilities for the Health, Safety and Safeguarding of the Members that arise from its very nature, Camp, and particularly residential Camp, must be very carefully organised. Rigorous Risk Assessments must be carried out at all venues to be used, and the person in charge of the Camp (the Camp Organiser) must be fully conversant with The Pony Club's Health and Safety Rule Book and Safeguarding Policy. Camp Organisers should be given guidance on supervision levels and safeguarding, particularly at night.

10.13 A responsible adult should be available to the Members at all times of the day and night. There should also be a trained First Aider equipped with a mobile telephone and an appropriately stocked First-Aid Kit. Arrangements for catering must ensure that all food hygiene regulations are fully met.

Competitions

10.14 A Branch may organise competitions in any of The Pony Club's sports. These competitions can either be restricted to the Branch's own Members, restricted to Pony Club Members or open to the general public. All competitions organised by Pony Club Branches shall be conducted under the Rules as printed in the applicable Sport Rule Book unless otherwise stated in the schedule of classes and regulations published for the competition.

10.15 If a Branch organises a competitive event that is open to Members of the Pony Club, but not to the general public, then the entry form must require a visiting competitor's Branch/Centre to be identified

10.16 Cash or other valuable prizes must no be given at Pony Club competitions. Prizes should normally take the form of rosettes ar or trophies.

Other Activities

10.17 A Branch can arrange other activities for its Members and their families such as a Quiz, outings, social events and fund-raising events. These other activities do not need to be equestrian in nature.

11. CENTRE AND CENTRE PLUS MEMBERSHIP

Purpose and Scope of Activities

11.1 Centre Membership is intended to enable someone who only rides a Centre owned horse/pony during a Centre organise activity to become a Member of The Pony Club. Centre Members are able to take part i all Pony Club activities.

11.2 Centre Plus Membership is for Membe who ride at a Centre and also have regular access to ride a horse/pony outside of Centre organised activities. As with all Pony Club memberships, third party liability insurance applies. The Centre Plus Membership fee wil be equal to the Branch Membership fee.

11.3 Centre Members and Centre Plus Members are eligible to participate in all sports and competitions open to Members, although the Centre Equitation competition for Centre Members only.

11.4 Centre and Centre Plus Members have third party legal liability insurance cover.

Membership – Centre and Centre Plus

11.5 The Trustees will set the rate for the Annual Subscription and will publish this in the Handbook.

11.6 The first Annual Subscription is due when first applying for membership. The initial membership application must be endorsed by the Centre Proprietor.

11.7 Membership runs for twelve months from the date the subscription is received. A renewal reminder will be sent to the Member one month before the end of his Membership Subscription Year. Email Renewal reminders will be sent to the Member in the month leading up to the end of the Membership Subscription Year.

11.8 The Centre Membership Committee may expel any Member whose conduct is such, in their opinion, as to be injurious to the character or reputation of The Pony Club, to any of its Centres or to the interests of The Pony Club or Members or whose conduct shall in the opinion of the Centre Membership Committee, make a Member unfit or unsuitable to continue as a Member.

11.9 Before the Centre Membership Committee expels a Member, they will be given reasonable notice of relevant meetings, full opportunity to defend themselves and to justify or explain their conduct. This will include making representations by way of defence, justification and explanation on behalf of the Member by the parents. If the majority of the Centre Membership Committee present at the inquiry are of the opinion that the Member has been guilty of the alleged conduct and that the Member or parents of such Member has or have failed to justify or explain it satisfactorily, the Centre Membership Committee shall ask the Member to resign. If they do not resign the Centre Membership Committee will expel the Member from The Pony Club.

11.10 The Pony Club Office may refuse to renew the membership of a Centre Member or Centre Plus Member. Reasons for such action would normally be given.

11.11 On the ending of membership, either because of age, non-payment of subscription, resignation, expulsion or any other reason whatsoever, the Member will forfeit all the privileges of membership and all rights against The Pony Club.

11.12 Subscriptions and/or fees will not in such circumstances be returnable and the Member will still be liable for all annual subscriptions and/or fees that had become due and remained unpaid at the date of ending of the membership.

Area Centre Coordinators

11.13 The duties and responsibilities of an Area Centre Coordinator are:

- To assess all riding schools who apply to become a Pony Club Centre and report their findings to The Pony Club Office.
- To contact each of the existing Pony Club Centres in their Area annually and report their findings to The Pony Club Office.
- To be a point of contact for the Centres in their Area for advice and assistance with Pony Club Tests and other aspects of Pony Club within the Centre.
- To liaise with the Area Representative
- To assist The Pony Club Office and Area Representative in communicating national or regional events, qualifying competitions and training opportunities to the Pony Club Centres.

Pony Club Centres

11.14 When a Riding Centre Proprietor applies to join the scheme, the Area Representative will be informed and the Riding Centre will be visited by an Area Centre Coordinator.

11.15 Provided that The Pony Club Office is satisfied that the Centre meets the required standards, the Centre Proprietor will be invited to enter into a legal agreement regulating the relationship between himself and The Pony Club. The Riding Centre will become known as The xxxxxx Pony Club Centre and its participation in the scheme will be renewable annually through an affiliation fee.

11.16 The Centre Membership Advisory Committee may recommend the withholding or termination a Centre's participation in the Centre Membership Scheme at any time if the Centre is unable to provide, or ceases to provide, the benefits of Centre Membership as determined in Rule Section 11.1 above, or ceases to meet the standards required by The Pony Club. Adequate notice will be given, along with reasons for withdrawal, in reasonable time.

11.17 Pony Club Centres will display a Pony Club Centre plaque.

11.18 All Pony Club Centres must hold a current licence under the Riding Establishments Acts 1964 and 1970 or The Riding Establishments Regulations (Northern Ireland) 1980 or The Animal Welfare (Licensing of Activities Involving Animals) (England) Regulations 2018 (as appropriate).

11.19 All Pony Club Centres must have current Public Liability Insurance Cover, which must include cover for all their Pony Club activities. Members riding Centre owned ponies will be covered by The Pony Club Third Party Legal Liability Insurance Policy when taking part in any Pony Club activity. However, the pony itself will not be covered by this Insurance.

11.20 Pony Club Centres are required to provide the benefits of membership, including mounted and dismounted instruction to Members.

Pony Club Tests at Pony Club Centres

11.21 The Centre Proprietor must contact his Area Centre Coordinator, Area Representative and/ or the local District Commissioner if necessary, in order to find suitable Assessors for the Test to be taken at E, D, D+, C or C+ Standard. Thereafter, the Proprietor must consult the Area Representative as to how and where further Tests are to be taken.

11.22 The riding component of the C Test must be taken outside and not in an indoor school.

11.23 It will be the responsibility of the Centre Proprietor to order any badges, felts, and certificates for presentation to successful candidates.

11.24 The Centre Proprietor or Test Organiser should update the Membership Database with badge and test results.

11.25 Candidates may be charged a fee by the Centre to cover the cost of Assessors' expenses, normal hire charges, and other costs.

12. REMUNERATION AND EXPENSES

Remuneration

12.1 No Trustee shall receive remuneration from The Pony Club in any circumstances. No Area Representative nor any District Commissioner shall receive any salary or emolument from The Pony Club or any of its Branches for performing his normal function within The Pony Club. However, the Management Committee shall have authority to waive this Rule for Area Representatives and District Commissioners in exceptional circumstances, in order to employ the particular skills of an individual for a specific purpose and provided that such payment is legally permissible.

12.2 Applications for such a waiver should be sent to the Chief Executive, in writing, giving precise details of the work to be done and the remuneration to be paid.

Payment of Coaches and others

12.3 Coaches and others such as Camp helpers may be paid a fee on production of an invoice. It is strongly recommended that fees should be negotiated in advance, and that they should not be paid in cash. Those paid fees may be members of Branch Committees but cannot be the District Commissioner unless he has received a dispensation from the Volunteers and Officials Committee under Rule 9.24.

Expenses

12.4 Travelling and out of pocket expenses of Trustees and, members of committees will be refunded by The Pony Club Office in accordance with the Pony Club Expenses Policy. Expense claims must be submitted to The Pony Club Office within 30 days from the end of the month of which the expense was incurred.

12.5 Branches may also reimburse such expenses incurred by District Commissioners, Branch Officers, Committee members and others acting on behalf of the Branch. Branches may, if they wish, pay a flat sum or a rate per capita to their District Commissioner, but they should be aware that the Inland Revenue may require the District Commissioner to justify the amount paid. Travelling expenses will be paid at either the Standard Class train fare or at the currently approved mileage rate if travelling by car. This rate should be used as the normal allowance for all Pony Club meetings and events. However, when using qualified officials (i.e. British Dressage judges or BS judges) their official rate should be paid.

13. THE PONY CLUB TESTS

13.1 Details regarding conditions of tests and badges can be found in the Administrative Notes section of the Handbook and online at pcuk.org.

13.2 Subject to rule 13.3, all mandatory tests must be taken in order.

13.3 In exceptional circumstances, an Area Representative, at the request of a District Commissioner or Centre Proprietor, may grant permission for a Member to omit taking a test before progressing to the next highest test.

14. COACH AND INSTRUCTOR ACCREDITATION

14.1 The Pony Club accredits its coaches and instructors in line with the detailed notes laid out in the "Coaches and Training" section of the Administrative Notes in the Handbook and on the website. The Pony Club grants this accreditation to coaches and instructors, and reserves the right to remove or suspend the accreditation of any coach or instructor if it considers it necessary. If a coach or instructor has their accreditation removed or suspended, they may not instruct for any Pony Club Branch or Centre until their accreditation is reinstated.

15. THE PONY CLUB CHAMPIONSHIPS

15.1 Each year, the Management Committee will appoint a Championships Committee to arrange a championship for each of the sports. Wherever possible, all of the sports will hold their championships at the same venue during one week in the second half of August, but it is recognised that some sports may have to hold their own separate championships.

Qualification for the championships will be through competitions held by each Area. In some sports, these Area competitions may be replaced or augmented by Zone competitions, in which two or more Areas combine.

15.2 The rules for each competition will be approved by the relevant committee for each sport.

16. DRESS AND SADDLERY FOR PONY CLUB MEMBERS

Hats

16.1 It is mandatory for all Members to wear a protective helmet at all times when mounted with a chinstrap fastened and adjusted so as to prevent movement of the hat in the event of a fall. This rule defines the quality of manufacture that is required. The individual sports also have additional requirements with regard to colour and type. It is strongly recommended that second hand hats are not purchased.

16.2 The current hat standards accepted by the Pony Club are detailed in the table below:

Hat Standard	Safety Mark	Allowed at the following activities:
PAS 015:1998 or 2011* with BSI Kitemark		All activities
VG1 with BSI Kitemark		All activities
Snell E2001* onwards with the official Snell label and number	E2001	All activities
ASTM-F1163 2004a onwards with the SEI mark	SEI	All activities
AS/NZS 3838 2006 onwards	Australian Standard AS/NZS Certified Product	All activities

In order to ensure riders are wearing the most up to date riding hats, please note that from the 1st January 2023, the following hat standards will no longer be accepted, due to the age of hats made to these standards:

1. PAS 015 1998

2. SNELL 2001

To manage this change, a new colour of h tag will be required for all BE, PC and BRC activities from 1st January 2023.

- For cross-country riding (over 80cm) including Eventing, Tetrathlon, Horse Trials, Pony Racing (whether it be tests, rallies, competition or training) and Mounted Games competitions, a jockey skull cap must be worn with no fixed peak, peak type extensions or noticeable protuberances above the eyes or to the front, and should have an even round or elliptical shape with a smooth or slightly abrasive surface, having no peak or peak type extensions. Noticeable protuberanc above the eyes or to the front not greate than 5mm, smooth and rounded in nature are permitted. A removable hat cover with a light flexible peak may be used if required.
- It is strongly recommended that a jockey skull cap is worn for cross-country riding over lower fences (less than 80cm) as there is research evidence that a fall onto the fixed peak can result in an over extension of the neck backwards with th potential for serious injury.
- No recording device is permitted (e.g. ha cameras) as they may have a negative effect on the performance of the hat in the event of a fall.
- The fit of the hat and the adjustment

of the harness are as crucial as the quality. Members are advised to try several makes to find the best fit. The hat should not move on the head when the head is tipped forward. Most helmet manufacturers recommend you visit a qualified BETA (British Equestrian Trade Association) fitter.

- Hats must be replaced after a severe impact as subsequent protection will be significantly reduced. Hats deteriorate with age and should be replaced after three to five years depending upon the amount of use.
- Hats must be worn at all times (including at prize-giving) when mounted with a chinstrap fastened and adjusted so as to prevent movement of the hat in the event of a fall.
- For Show Jumping and Mounted Games the cover, if applicable, shall be dark blue, black or brown only.
- For Dressage, hats and hat covers must be predominately black, navy blue or a conservative dark colour that matches the rider's jacket for Area competitions or above. The Pony Club Hat silk is also acceptable.
- The Official Steward / Organiser may, at his discretion, eliminate a competitor riding in the area of the competition without a hat or with the chinstrap unfastened or with a hat that does not comply with these standards.

Hat Checks and Tagging

16.3 The Pony Club and its Branches and Linked Centres will appoint Officials, who are familiar with The Pony Club hat rule, to carry out hat checks and tag each hat that complies with the requirements set out in the hat rule with an aquamarine Pony Club hat tag.

16.4 Hats fitted with an aquamarine Pony Club, British Eventing (BE) or British Riding Club (BRC) hat tag will not need to be checked on subsequent occasions. However, the Pony Club reserves the right to randomly spot check any hat regardless of whether it is already tagged.

16.5 Pony Club hat tags are only available to purchase from The Pony Club Shop.

16.6 Tagging indicates that a hat meets the accepted standards, NO check of the fit and condition of the hat is implied. It is considered the responsibility of the Member's parent(s) / guardian(s) to ensure that their hat complies with the required standards and is tagged before they go to any Pony Club event. Also, they are responsible for ensuring that the manufacturer's guidelines with regard to fit and replacement are followed.

Ties and Stocks

16.7 The Pony Club's colours are pale blue, gold and purple, and Members should wear the approved tie in these colours whenever attending a Pony Club activity, unless the wearing of a tie is inappropriate to that activity.

16.8 Recognising the wide age range of Members, there is also a dark blue tie, which may be worn by Members who have attained their 18th birthday. Alternatively, a plain white or cream stock may be worn with a black or navy jacket, or a coloured stock may be worn with a tweed hacking jacket. It is permitted to wear a Pony Club stock with any coloured jacket.

Badges

16.9 The official membership badge should be worn at all Pony Club activities when a jacket is worn.

16.10 Branches and Centres give Members a coloured felt showing the highest Test standard achieved by the Member. It should be worn behind the membership badge.

16.11 Cloth Achievement Badges should be sown on to the Branch or Centre sweatshirt.

Body Protectors

16.12 The Pony Club does not make the use of body protectors compulsory, except for all Cross Country riding and Pony Racing whether it be training or competition. If worn for any Pony Club activity a Body Protector must meet BETA 2009 Level 3 standard (purple label) or BETA 2018 Level 3 standard (blue and black label).

16.13 For general use, the responsibility for choosing body protectors and the decision as to their use must rest with Members and their parents. It is recommended that a rider's body protector should not be more than 2% of their body weight. When worn, body protectors must fit correctly, be comfortable and must not restrict movement. BETA recommends body protectors are replaced at least every three to five years, after which the impact absorption properties of the foam may have started to decline.

16.14 BETA 2009 Level3 (purple label) body protectors will continue to be accepted at Pony Club competitions until 31st December 2024.

16.15 Riders who choose to use the Woof Wear Body Cage EXO must lodge a key with the Event Organiser when they collect their number.

Air Jackets

16.16 When an air jacket inflates the sudden noise startles horses in the immediate vicinity thereby causing difficulties for the other members of a ride if used in a group ride in a confined area, e.g. an indoor school or outdoor manège. Air jackets are therefore no encouraged for group rides.

16.17 If a rider chooses to wear an air jacket i Cross Country or Pony Racing, it must only b used in addition to a normal body protector which meets the BETA 2009 Level 3 standard (purple label) or BETA 2018 Level 3 standard (blue and black label). Parents and Members must be aware that riders may be permitted to continue after a fall in both competition and training rides for Cross Country and/or Pony Racing, provided the rider has been passed as fit to continue by First Aid Provider In the event of a fall, it must be fully deflated or removed before continuing, after which, th conventional body protector will continue to give protection. Air jackets must not be worn under a jacket and number bibs should be fitted loosely or with elasticised fastenings over the air jacket.

Medical Armbands

16.18 Medical armbands are advised if Members are not accompanied by a responsible adult, including hacking on roads and are compulsory for Pony Racing and for Endurance rides.

Clothing, Footwear and Stirrups

16.19 When mounted at Pony Club activities, Members should wear a riding jacket or Branch/Centre sweatshirt, jodhpurs with leather shoes or jodhpur boots or breeches and either leather or rubber riding boots, a suitable plain-coloured shirt with a collar and The Pony Club tie or a stock.

16.20 Only standard riding or jodhpur boots with a well-defined square cut heel may be worn. No other footwear will be permitted including wellington boots, yard boots, country boots, "muckers" or trainers. Boots with interlocking treads are not permitted, nor are the boots or treads individually. Laces on boots must be taped for Mounted Games only.

16.21 Plain black or brown half chaps may be worn with jodhpur boots of the same colour. Tassels and fringes are not allowed.

16.22 Stirrups should be of the correct size to suit the rider's boots. They must have 7mm (¼") clearance on either side of the boot. To find this measurement, tack checkers should move the foot across to one side of the stirrup, with the widest part of the foot on the tread. From the side of the foot to the edge of the stirrup should be 14mm.

There are now many types of stirrups marketed as "safety stirrups". All riders must ensure that their stirrups are suitable for their type of footwear, the activities in which they take part and that the stirrup leathers are in good condition.

16.23 There are no prescribed weight limits on metal stirrups. However, with the advent of stirrups of other materials, weight limits are seen to be given by manufacturers. Anyone who buys these stirrups should take particular note if weight limits are on the box or on the attached information leaflets.

16.24 Neither the feet, nor the stirrup leathers nor irons, may be attached to the girth, nor may the feet be attached to the stirrup irons.

It is strongly recommended that the design of the stirrup chosen allows the foot to be released easily in the event of a rider fall. Specific rules for individual sports can be found in the respective sports rulebooks.

Particular focus should be on ensuring that the boot and stirrup are the correct size for the rider taking part and used in line with the manufacturer's guidance.

For the avoidance of doubt, at Pony Club events:

- **stirrups which connect the boot and the stirrup magnetically are not allowed**
- **Interlocking boot soles and stirrup treads are not allowed**

16.25 New clothing is not expected, but what is worn must be clean, neat and tidy. Jeans should not be worn when mounted except when specifically allowed by certain sports. Polo shirts in Branch colours are allowed at rallies and at camp.

Spurs

16.26 Spurs may be worn at Rallies and other events. Any misuse of spurs will be reported to the District Commissioner/Centre Proprietor, Area Representative and Training Chairman and riders who are reported will be recorded and monitored. Sharp spurs are not permitted. Only blunt spurs, without rowels or sharp edges, and spurs that have a smooth rotating ball on the shank may be worn.
If the spurs are curved, the curve must be downwards and the shank must point straight to the back and not exceed 4 cm in length. The measurement is taken from the heel of the boot to the end of the shank.

Jewellery

16.27 For safety reasons jewellery, other than medical jewellery, a wristwatch, a wedding ring, a stock pin worn horizontally or a tie clip, is not allowed. It is recommended that stock pins are removed for cross country. Members who are contemplating piercing their ears or any other part of their body should be aware that they will not be allowed to participate in any Pony Club mounted equestrian activities until such time as the "sleepers" can safely be removed. The reason for this is that sleepers have in the past caused injuries following falls. This rule will be strictly enforced.

EXCEPTION: In the event of a person being unable to remove permanent jewellery, it must be adequately protected by being covered by a sticking plaster or another appropriate material prior to presenting at tack check. **The wearing of such jewellery while competing is at the risk of the Member/parent/guardian.**

Competitions

16.28 Additional or different dress requirements for competitions may be specified in the Sport Rule Books, but otherwise, these Rules shall apply.

Saddlery

16.29 Side reins, grass reins and balance support reins are permitted to be used at rallies and general Pony Club activities. Side reins must be loosely fitted and clipped on from the bit to the 'd' ring. The height limit for jumping is 50cms. Other than this only saddlery permitted in the Sport Rule Books may be used at Rallies and general Pony Club activities relating to that sport.

Unsafe Tack

All tack must be clean, in a good state of repair, properly fitted and suitable for purpose. Tack inspections are routinely carried out at events and the organisers may prohibit participation in the event if they consider the tack to be inadequate or unsuitable. Specific sport rules are detailed in respective rulebooks.

Electronic Devices

Electronic devices (i.e. headphones, mobile phones, etc. enabling another person to communicate with the rider) are not allowed whilst the rider is competing. No recording device is permitted (e.g. hat/ bridle cameras, etc).

17. SAFEGUARDING

17.1 The Pony Club believes that it is essential that children and young people are encouraged to take part in outdoor activitie and sports as part of their development to adulthood. Their participation in sport must be in a secure, safe and fun environment an be protected from harm. The positive effects of involvement with horses can help develop self-esteem, teamwork and leadership. This can only take place if equestrian sport is effectively regulated and managed by well trained staff and volunteers.

17.2 The full Safeguarding Policy contains the necessary policies and procedures which should be implemented and adhered to, including but not limited to:

- The appointment of a Branch/Centre Safeguarding Officer
- Dealing with safeguarding concerns and allegations
- Safer recruitment practices, including requirements for those carrying out regulated activity/work

17.3 As a member body of British Equestria (BEF), in applying our Safeguarding Policy, we will follow the BEF Case Management Policy (with any necessary modifications). Th Policy includes a provision allowing for the temporary suspension of an individual durin an investigation.

18. DISPLAYS

18.1 Branches will not give displays, or stage competitions, at shows or other public gatherings without first obtaining the permission of their Area Representative.

19. PROHIBITED ACTIVITIES

19.1 Because of the risks involved, team-chasing events or practices must not be organised by The Pony Club, nor should Branch teams be entered in such events. The same restriction applies to Racing, other than racing sanctioned by The Pony Club Racing Committee. Team-chasing and other unauthorized racing is not covered by Pony Club insurance.

20. COMPLAINTS PROCEDURE

Competition Complaints and Objections

20.1 Complaints and objections arising from within competitions should be dealt with in accordance with the procedure detailed in the relevant sport rule book. Decisions made in this way are final, and no appeal will be entertained. Should a breach of eligibility subsequently be discovered, then the Sport Committee may disqualify the offending team or individual. If the said individual was a member of a qualifying team, and their score contributes to the qualification, the team will be disqualified unless the qualification holds up using the discard score. In the event of disqualification, the next best placed team or individual will be promoted. Decisions made by the Sport Committee shall be final. No issue of eligibility can be considered after the Championship competition has been held.

Other Complaints and Problems

20.2 If a problem arises within a Branch or a Centre, it is for the District Commissioner or Area Centre Coordinator to try initially to resolve the problem. If they are unable to do so, then they should enlist the help of the Area Representative, who will consult with the relevant Committee Chairmen if necessary. If the problem still cannot be resolved, then the Area Representative (with the assistance of a Branch Operations Director if required) will refer the matter to the Rules and Compliance Committee, whose decision will, subject to Rule 20.3 be final. The decision will be advised to the complainant in writing.

20.3 The Rules and Compliance Committee may in exceptional circumstances and in cases where the Committee is unable to determine the matter properly due to a conflict of interest arising must, ask the Vice Chairman to establish an Appeals Committee under Rule 4.30 to review the matter and make a decision on it.

20.4 Any appeal to the Appeals Committee will be considered only after the above procedure has been carried out. If the complainant wishes to lodge an appeal, they must do so within 28 days of the date of the decision letter. They must also pay a deposit to The Pony Club Office. This deposit will be refunded if the appeal is upheld. The amount of the deposit will be shown in the Handbook.

21. FINANCE

21.1 Branches shall be largely autonomous in their control of Branch funds. However, it should be understood that, under charity law, the funds of The Pony Club, whether they are held by the Branches or by The Pony Club Office, are all part of The Charity. This means that, if any part of The Pony Club cannot pay its debts, payment must be made from elsewhere in The Pony Club. For this reason, a Branch may not, without the approval of the Finance Committee, enter into a financial commitment that risks a loss of a sum which is greater than £5,000 or the sum equal to 50% of its free reserves at the time of the commitment, whichever is the lesser amount.

21.2 A Branch that wishes to assign Designated Funds must obtain the consent of the Finance Committee.

21.3 Any purchase or rental of land (irrespective of value), and any capital expenditure in excess of £10,000, requires the prior approval of the Trustees. This requirement does not apply to casual hiring of facilities, provided that the hire period does not exceed one month. A Branch does not have the legal capacity to buy or rent land or buildings in its own name. All such transactions must be in the name of "The Pony Club", with the interest of the Branch being noted. All costs incurred, such as legal fees, are to be paid by the Branch.

21.4 Legally, The Pony Club is a charitable company, governed by its Memorandum and

Articles of Association. In order to comply with the Memorandum and Articles, Pony Club funds may only be deposited with or lent to an institution, such as a bank or building society, which is regulated by the Financial Conduct Authority.

21.5 Bank Accounts

- Branches should use online banking provided that the Bank has a feature that requires two separate people to authorise transactions. For branches where this is not currently possible they should transition to a new account. In the interim paper statements should be obtained at least monthly and presented at every branch meeting.
- As a minimum, the Treasurer and District Commissioner should be signatories on the account. It is recommended that other officers are also made signatories in order that payments are not held up due to unavailability of the Treasurer or District Commissioner.
- The Treasurer and District Commissioner should review the account regularly and at least monthly
- All bank payments, both online and paper cheques require two signatories.
- Disbursements may not be made by telephone banking.
- Debit cards may be used but the Treasurer may not be the holder of a Debit Card. All holders must give the transaction dockets to the Treasurer at not greater than monthly intervals, together with an explanation of the reason for each purchase. The Treasurer will review these and report any anomalies to the District Commissioner or Area Representative.
- Credit cards are not allowed.

Building Society Account

If the Branch has a building society account, the Treasurer must bring the pass book to every committee meeting and make it available for inspection and must get the balance updated as at the year end.

21.6 These rules relate to all sub-groups, such as Parents' Associations and Sports Sub-committees that belong to the Branch.

Online Payment Systems

21.7 The use of online payment systems such as PayPal, Worldpay, Sagepay by Branches is permitted. However, it should be used in accordance with the relevant rules laid out in The Pony Club's Treasurer Guidelines, which are available on the Treasurers and Finance section of the website.

Returns to The Pony Club Office

21.8 To comply with charity law, all Branches are required to submit an Annual Financial Return to the Pony Club Office by 28th February following the end of The Pony Club Year. Failure to do this will result in fines being imposed on The Pony Club, which will be recharged to the Branch(es) concerned. Invoices will be raised for any fines and sent to the branch pcuk.org email address.

21.9 The funds of all sub-branches, Parents' Associations and other sub-groups must be reported, either separately, or consolidated with the Branch. Funds held by Areas will also be reported.

21.10 Memberships are processed both centrally at the Pony Club Office and by the Branch on Pelham. At the end of each month a payment will be taken from or made to the Branch bank account by Direct Debit in respect of memberships taken during the month. Branches must ensure that a Direct Debit mandate is in place and kept up to date. Changes must be notified to the Pony Club Office.

21.11 For the purposes of the capitation returns and the capitation fees, a Member who transfers from one Branch to another during The Pony Club Year shall be reported by the Branch to which he has paid his subscription. He should be excluded completely from the Return of the other Branch. Capitation is paid at the joining Branch and no subsequent adjustment can be made.

21.12 The annual financial return is due by the specified due date. Late submissions will incur a 'late submission fee'. If it is still outstanding one month after the specified due date, a further late submission fee will be incurred.

The fee(s) will be published in the Handbook or on the website. The invoice for the fee will be addressed to the District Commissioner of the Branch or for Area returns the relevant Area Representative and will be sent to the their respective @pcuk.org email address.

A completed Branch Annual Financial Return submission will encompass:

- Fully completed, balanced return including a completed declaration signed by the Treasurer
- Bank statements and building society pass books showing the balance as at 31st December
- Fixed Asset Register

21.13 If the return is not received within 28 days from the date of the invoice for the fine, the Branch and/or one or more of its Officers or Committee members may be suspended from membership of The Pony Club until such time the Return is received. If a Return or Report has to be returned to a Branch because it contains errors, the Branch will remain in default until the satisfactorily corrected Return or Report (together with any payment that may be due) is received at The Pony Club Office. The Pony Club Office can also withhold future Direct Credits until payment is received.

The Chairman of The Pony Club has discretion to waive this Rule if he is satisfied that there are sufficient extenuating circumstances.

21.14 Following consultation with the Area Representative, the Management Committee may impose different reporting requirements upon Branches that are persistently late in filing their Returns.

21.15 It is a requirement of The Pony Club insurers that a list of the Members covered by public liability insurance can be made available to them if required. To satisfy this requirement, all Branches must submit details of their current membership by means of the online Database.

21.16 In the event that a Branch is unable to complete its Annual Financial return it may request the Pony Club Office to undertake the task for it. If a Branch makes such a request it must supply to the Pony Club Office: -

- A completed and balanced cashbook in either electronic or hard copy
- Copies of all bank statements for the year

If a branch does not have a cash book there will be an additional charge payable by the branch.

21.17 If a request is made to the Pony Club Office to complete an Annual Financial return the Branch will pay to the Pony Club Office a fee calculated in accordance with the following: -

- If the request is made prior to 16th February a fee of £5.00 per Member
- If the request is made on or after 16th February a fee of £7.50 per Member

An additional charge of £5.00 per member will be incurred to complete the cashbook.

Record Keeping

21.18 It is the responsibility of the Branch Treasurer to keep appropriate financial records. This must include:

- All financial transactions must be recorded in the cashbook (electronic / hardcopy), this includes recording the VAT that has been paid on each payment as

per the receipt
- All payments made must have a receipt (can be scanned)
- Accounts packages such as Sage, Xero etc can be used
- All expenses claimed must have appropriate receipts attached

All records must be kept for a period of 6 years

Branch Audits

21.19 The Pony Club Office may at any time request to audit the last two years of the Annual Financial Return of a Branch. Within 30 days of receiving an audit request the Branch Treasuer must send to the Pony Club Office the following documents: -

- Monthly Bank statements for all bank accounts held by the Branch for the period requested
- Download of all online payment platform transactions during the period requested
- A copy of the cashbook
- All receipts to evidence expenditure

21.20 Results of the audit will be communicated back to the Branch District Commissioner and Area Representative.

Branch Correspondence

21.21 In order to comply with GDPR requirements, all correspondence with a Branch will be undertaken through the (branchname)@ pcuk.org email address and the District Commissioner must ensure that this email is monitored at regular intervals sufficient to ensure that all relevant correspondence is dealt with expeditiously. To this end, the District Commissioner may share the password with anyone he deems relevant to have access to the email address.

Refunds

21.22 No refunds after close of entries.

21.23 Withdrawal before close of entries on production of vet / medical certificate will get a full refund less a £10 admin fee (to be retained by The Organiser).

21.24 In the event of a competition being abandoned, for whatever reason, a refund of 50% of the entry fee will be given (0% for Po

21.25 Cash

- In order to mitigate the risk associated with holding cash, cash transactions should be kept to a minimum.
- All cash handled by staff and volunteers must be dealt with so as to ensure its safe custody and mitigate against loss whether through fraud, misappropriatic or mistake.
- All payments made in cash must be supported by a receipt or other form of documentation to support the payment must be recorded in a petty cash book and should be reviewed and authorised by someone other than the person who maintaining the petty cash.
- A record of all cash received should be made in the petty cash book along with sufficient detail.
- Receipts should be issued for all cash received into petty cash. For fund raising activities such as raffles, one receipt for the total amount is sufficient but the receipt should detail the activity and individual giving the money.
- A regular and independent check of the petty cash float and records must be undertaken.

Direct Debits and Direct Credits

21.26

- Branches must maintain an up to date Direct Debit Mandate and must notify th Pony Club Office of any amendments
- Branches will be notified of payments being made to the Branch or payments being made by the Branch relating to subscriptions and invoices raised by The Pony Club Office at least 10 days prior to the payment being made / taken.

- Any payments which are not regarding membership will have been invoiced in the month prior to the payment being taken and will have been sent to the branch pcuk.org email.

21.27 In order to safeguard individuals and to protect the funds of the Pony Club , the Branch Committee/District Commissioner shall ensure that controls are in place to mitigate the risk of loss of the assets of the branch (whether through fraud, misappropriation or mistake).

22. INSURANCE

22.1 The Pony Club has Insurance under a number of headings and policies, a summary of which is provided in the Handbook. In particular, all Branch and Centre Members are covered for their legal liability for accidental injury or damage to third parties or their property, arising out of the use or ownership of ponies at any time, not just on Pony Club activities. A full policy summary is shown on The Pony Club website under Parents Info.

22.2 Members and their parents must read the summary of cover carefully, to ensure that it satisfies their own requirements. It must be understood that this is liability Insurance and does not cover property belonging to, or in the care of, the Member or his family. Nor does it cover injury to the Member or his family. To comply with insurance requirements, all employees of The Pony Club (including contractors), paid and unpaid officials, instructors, volunteers, parents, Members of The Pony Club and visitors must: -

- Take all reasonable care for the Health and Safety and Welfare of themselves and others that may be affected by their actions or omissions.
- Co-operate fully with The Pony Club and its Officials on all Health and Safety and Safeguarding issues.
- Not intentionally or recklessly interfere with or misuse anything provided in the interests of Health and Safety.
- Use correctly and as intended all work items, procedures and personal protective equipment provided by The Pony Club (or other employers), in accordance with the training and instructions given and report any loss or defect immediately.
- Inform the District Commissioner or activity organiser of any situation they consider represents danger or could result in harm to themselves or others.
- Inform the District Commissioner or activity organiser of any failings or shortcomings as regards Health and Safety and Welfare.
- Report accidents either by making an entry in The Pony Club Accident Book or by informing the District Commissioner or activity organiser.

22.3 Insurance claims made by Branches are subject to an insurance excess, this excess may be recharged back to the Branch. This is £1,000.

23. LEGAL LIABILITY

23.1 Save for the death or personal injury caused by the negligence of the organisers, or anyone for whom they are in law responsible, neither the organisers of this event or The Pony Club nor any agent, employee or representative of these bodies, nor the landlord or his tenant, accepts any liability for any accident, loss, damage, injury or illness to horses, owners, riders, spectators, land, cars, their contents and accessories, or any other person or property whatsoever. Entries are only accepted on this basis.

24. GENERAL

24.1 Every eventuality cannot be provided for in these Rules. In any unforeseen or exceptional circumstances, it is the duty of the relevant officials to make a decision in the spirit and ethos of The Pony Club and to adhere as nearly as possible to the intention of these Rules.

Administrative Notes

PURPOSE

The Pony Club is a voluntary youth organisation for young people interested in ponies and riding. It has Branches and Centres worldwide but these notes apply only to the United Kingdom of Great Britain and Northern Ireland. Within the UK, it is a Registered Charity, and is subject to Charity legislation and to regulation by the Charity Commission.

The Pony Club's Charitable Purpose is:

- To promote and advance the education and understanding of the public and particularly children and young people, in all matters relating to horsemanship and the horse.
- To encourage the development of sportsmanship, unlocking potential by building resilience, confidence, teamwork and leadership skills.
- To support and develop the volunteering network to strengthen The Pony Club community and sustain life-long engagement with equestrianism.

The Pony Club has been granted constituent Membership of the National Council of Voluntary Organisations (NCVO). This means that The Pony Club is officially recognised as a National Youth Organisation.

The Pony Club is affiliated to the British Equestrian Federation.

The Pony Club Office is at **Lowlands Equestrian Centre, Old Warwick Road, Warwick, CV35 7AX,** where The Pony Club is managed by a permanent staff responsible to The Board of Trustees.

THE PONY CLUB LOGO

The logo is a registered Trade Mark and shou not be altered in any way without the expres permission of The Pony Club. The Pony Club logo should not be incorporated, integrated c positioned so closely to any other logo/s that appears to be part of that or those logos.

It is very important that, as a Branch or Centr representing The Pony Club, you are using an up to date good resolution logo, in order to show that the Branch / Centre is an official representation of the brand.

Copies of the logo and guidance are available on request to Branches and Centres via The Pony Club website, where you can request th specific type of logo you require.

PONY CLUB COLOURS

Full details of The Pony Club colour palette and how to use them for home and professional printing can be found in the brand guidelines document on The Pony Clu website.

PONY CLUB BADGES AND TIES

Members can buy badges and ties from thei Branch or Centre or from Pony Club Shop. Th official Membership badge should be worn a all Pony Club activities when a jacket is worn. The badge should be worn at Branch / Centr rallies, Shows, Branch or Centre Competition Area Competitions and at the Championship

It should be worn on the left lapel of the jacket. For safety reasons, it must be at least 4cm below the collar bone. A coloured felt showing the highest Test standard achieved by the Member is given to Members by their Branch or Centre. It should be worn behind the Membership badge. Sewn-on badges denoting the Test colours are also available up to B Test for Members wishing to wear them on their sweatshirts or at times when the Members badge is not worn.

Officials' Badges – The officials' badges have the same Pony Club design with a coloured enamel scroll attached bearing the title.

- **Trustee**
  Badge has a chrome surround with blue scroll
- **Area Representative**
  Badge has a chrome surround with a red scroll
- **Sport Chairmen**
  Badge has a chrome surround with blue scroll
- **District Commissioner**
  Badge has a chrome surround with a dark blue scroll
- **Assistant District Commissioner**
  Pale blue scroll
- **Branch Secretary**
  Red scroll
- **Local Committee**
  Dark blue scroll
- **Branch President**
  Dark blue scroll
- **Branch Chief Instructor**
  Green Scroll
- **Instructor's Bar**
  Blue bar bearing the word, Instructor
- **Health & Safety Officer**
  Dark green scroll
- **Treasurer**
  Grey scroll
- **Volunteer**
  White oval

From the point of view of third party insurance, officials are advised to wear the appropriate badge while acting in an official capacity for The Pony Club.

PRESS AND MARKETING

It is in the interests of The Pony Club that its aims and activities are kept in the public eye. Press Releases of Branch and Centre events and invitations can be sent to local press for events. Reports of events should be sent to newspapers immediately after they have taken place. The local BBC and independent radio and television stations are often interested in The Pony Club's activities and you can find templates and information on **the officials area of pcuk.org** to help you with this type of promotion. If Members are to participate in a radio or television programme, Branches and Centres must inform The Pony Club Office.

MARKETING MATERIALS

The Marketing department can be contacted through The Pony Club Office for any help or advice you may need, and also welcome input into additional resources.

PONY CLUB OFFICIAL CLOTHING

Pony Club clothing is available from **Wainwright Screenprint.**

PONY CLUB PUBLICATIONS

The Pony Club publishes a number of books and e-books on The Pony Club's teaching which are available from **Wainwright Screenprint.**

HEALTH AND SAFETY AND SAFEGUARDING

The requirements are decided by The Trustees with advice from the Health and Safety and Safeguarding Advisory Committee. These are published in the Health and Safety Rule Book and Safeguarding Policy (which can be found on the Pony Club website).

The Health and Safety Rulebook includes the following areas:

Risk Assessments

Risk assessment is the cornerstone of good health and safety management and is a vital tool in preventing and/or reducing the risk of injuries. The Pony Club approach to risk assessment is simple, we ask:

- **'How can someone get injured?'; and,**
- **'What are we going to do about it?'**

Documented risk assessments must be carried out and recorded for all Pony Club activities and events attended by Members. All areas of a venue/site that everyone has access to should considered, not just the riding activity or area. Guidelines for the completion of risk assessments and templates are available on the Pony Club website.

Medical and First Aid

There are recommended minimum levels of first aid cover for Pony Club activities and competitions (see First Aid Provision Matrix). The level of medical cover should be considered as part of the risk assessment. Further details can be found in the Health and Safety Rulebook and on The Pony Club website.

Accident Reporting

All incidents must be reported to Howden Group Insurance, **via the online accident report form.** The full process and link to form are available on the website.

Safeguarding Committment

The Pony Club believes that it is essential that children and young people are encouraged to take part in outdoor activities and sports as part of their development to adulthood. The participation in sport must be in a secure, safe and fun environment and be protected from harm. The positive effects of involveme with horses can help develop self-esteem, teamwork and leadership. This can only take place if equestrian sport is effectively regulated and managed by well trained staf and Volunteers.

Safeguarding Policy Statement

The Pony Club has a statutory duty to protect children and safeguard their welfare. Participants in Pony Club activiti are entitled to expect a safe and enjoyabl environment. The Pony Club policies and procedures are consistent with the Britis Equestrian (BEF) Safeguarding Policies.

The Safeguarding Policy includes the following areas:

- **Duty of care and responsibilities**
- **How to deal with concerns and allegations**
- **Safer recruitment practices**

INSURANCE

The Pony Club has a comprehensive portfoli of insurance, designed to give protection to the Association and its Members (including Centre Members), Branches, Volunteers and Employees. The insurances are arranged by The Pony Club's broker – Howden, One Creechurch Place, London, EC3A 5AF Tel: 020 7645 9339. Amongst the most importan policies are the liability policies. It should be noted that the liability insurances deal with claims made against The Pony Club or Members on a legal liability basis and not a moral liability basis.

The Pony Club Public Liability Insurance

This policy covers claims made against The Pony Club or a Pony Club Branch (based in Great Britain and Northern Ireland) or a person acting on their behalf arising out of the usual activities of The Pony Club or a Branch anywhere in the world. It covers accidental bodily injury to members of the public or damage to their property as a result of negligence. The limit of indemnity is thirty million pounds (£30M) in respect of any one occurrence.

Only normal Pony Club activities are automatically included – if a Branch wishes to engage in an activity outside of the normal activities for a Branch they should notify The Pony Club Office who will consult with insurers if necessary.

If a Branch is asked to provide an indemnity (perhaps by the owner of land that will be used by the Branch for an activity), the wording of any such indemnity must be referred to The Pony Club, **Lowlands Equestrian Centre, Old Warwick Road, Warwick, CV35 7AX** Tel: 02476 698300. Email: enquiries@pcuk.org: for approval before it is signed by the District Commissioner.

This policy will deal only with claims made against The Pony Club or Branches by third parties and will not cover damage to property belonging to The Pony Club or a Pony Club Branch or property in their care, custody or control. If cover is required for damage to property you should arrange separate insurance.

The Pony Club Employers' Liability Insurance

This policy covers claims made by employees against The Pony Club or Branch (based in Great Britain or Northern Ireland) arising out of the usual activities of The Pony Club or Branch anywhere in Great Britain, Northern Ireland, the Channel Islands or the Isle of Man (extended to world-wide for temporary visits by employees). It covers accidental bodily injury to any employee including any casual labourer such as a coach. The limit of indemnity is ten million pounds (£10M) in respect of any one occurrence but five million pounds (£5M) for terrorism or asbestos claims.

The Pony Club Members' Personal Liability Insurance

This policy covers claims made against the Member for accidental bodily injury to members of the public or damage to their property arising out of the Member's use or ownership or control of a horse or pony or horse/pony-drawn vehicle at any time – not just at Pony Club activities. Also covered are other persons using the Member's horse or pony or horse/pony-drawn vehicle with the Member's permission, unless such person is insured elsewhere. Cover is restricted to accidents occurring within the United Kingdom or Republic of Ireland

The Member's liability policy is one of 'last resort'. Therefore if any other policy is in place which would cover the claim, the alternative policy will respond before The Pony Club policy. Many household or equine mortality policies will include public liability cover and this will be explored before a claim is accepted under The Pony Club policy.

If the Member is a child and is too young to be found legally liable, then the policy will cover the parent or guardian of the Member for liability arising out of the Member's activities as provided for in the policy. Temporary Members are covered whilst attending Pony Club activities (from time of arrival until time of departure) only if they are attending a rally with a view to joining The Pony Club. This applies to a couple of rallies only.

The limit of indemnity is thirty million pounds (£30M) in respect of any one occurrence.

The policy does not cover:

- accidental bodily injury to the Member or anyone in the Members family, household or employ or damage to any such person's property or property in their care, custody or control.
- accidents occurring whilst the Member is engaged in racing, point to point, steeplechasing, team chasing or any other form of racing other than Endurance Riding or Official Pony Club Race Days and Training Days.
- accidents arising out of any business activities or the use of the Member's horse or pony or horse/pony-drawn vehicle for hire and reward.
- The first £250 of any claim for property damage.

For any queries relating to Pony Club insurance please contact:
Catherine Morgan
Catherine.morgan@howdengroup.com
Tel: 020 7645 9339

An Insurance Product Information Document for The Pony Club Members cover can be printed from pcuk.org under Join Us > Parents Information > Members Insurance

MEMBERSHIP

Branch Membership

Subscriptions (See Rule 8 For Definitions)

	Individual Member	Family Membership (as defined in rule 8.6)	Non-Riding Member
Full Year	**£82**	**£205**	**£37**
Capitation	£62	£154	£28

Late Submission Fees

Branches incurring late submission fees as specified in Rule 21.12 will be charged at the following rates:

- Overdue: £2.00 per Member
- One month overdue: an additional £3.00 per Member

The Membership shall be calculated on the reported Membership of the Branch for the preceding Pony Club year.

Appeals

In accordance with Rule 20.4 of The Pony Club, the deposit required to lodge an appea will be £100.00.

Forming a New Branch

Any person wishing to form a new Branch should consult the Area Representative for advice and guidance.

Centre Membership

	Centre Member	Centre Plus Member
Full Year	**£37**	**£82**
Centre Incentive	£2.50	£5.50

COACHES AND TRAINING

The Pony Club aims to offer the best possible coaching and opportunities to its members a all levels.

Learning about the care and welfare of horse and ponies is paramount to Pony Club ethos. Through working rallies, training, and camps our members can progress in their riding and care knowledge using our achievement badges and efficiency tests to help them develop their skills.

Having a Pony Club rally organiser or lead coach is strongly recommended, they will work alongside the District Commissioner. The District Commissioner should always be available to answer queries and discuss problems which may arise. There is a badge for the lead coach which can be given by the District Commissioner or Centre Proprietor. The lead coach must have attended a Pony Club Continuing Professional Development (CPD) course. The lead coach may be a member of the Branch / Centre Committee, and is responsible for:

- Arranging the instructional programme for rallies and camp (using the syllabus of coaching in the Coach's Folder is recommended).
- Ensuring that facilities are risk assessed before use and that the equipment is ready for each rally/camp.
- Approve coaches for rallies and be able to brief the coach accordingly.
- Finding coaches with specialised knowledge.
- Organising meetings and practical sessions for coaches and ensure that all coach requirements are up to date.
- Advising coaches on suitable CPD courses.
- Organise any relevant training relating to Branch or Centre team selection.
- Assist in the preparation of members wishing to take their efficiency tests.

Coaches' Courses

The Pony Club believes that part of its mission is to train its own future coaches. Potential coaches come from all age groups but particularly from older members who have had the benefit of being part of The Pony Club community. The Training Committee recommends a specific route for new coaches without a formal equestrian coaching qualification which is the Introduction to Pony Club Coaching Steps 1-3 Courses.

For a course to count as a CPD course, it must be notified to The Pony Club Office, for inclusion on the website at least three weeks in advance of the course date. Courses may be run by any Branch, Centre, or Area, with the approval of the Area Representative. Guidance on what courses to offer can be found on The Pony Club website.

The Pony Club Manual of Horsemanship

The Manual is a complete basic guide to horsemanship and riding. Currently in its updated 14th edition it is a worldwide bestseller, containing information on a wide range of equestrian topics. The manual should be used as the basis for all instruction to members.

Coaching

One of the objectives of The Pony Club is to offer instruction and coaching sessions which enable members to develop both their riding and understanding of equine care. Coaches must base their teaching on The Pony Club Manual of Horsemanship and Instructor's Handbook to avoid conflicting methods. Pony Club coaches are divided into categories according to their use and role within The Pony Club. It is a requirement that all coaches used by The Pony Club are listed as active coaches on PELHAM. Further information can be found on The Pony Club website. Coaches without an up to date Enhanced DBS or Safeguarding certificate must not be used.

The Pony Club Efficiency Tests

Test fees can be found on the website.

Test Colours

A coloured disc or felt (obtainable by Branches and Centres from The Pony Club Shop) will be issued to members to denote the test standard of efficiency achieved. The disc or felt representing the highest test achieved by the member should be worn behind the membership badge. Successful candidates are also awarded a certificate in the appropriate colour.

The colours should be awarded as follows: -

- E – Pale Yellow
- D - Yellow
- D+ - White
- C (Horse & Pony Care) - Meadow Green
- C (Riding) - Silver Grey
- C both sections - Green
- C+ (Horse & Pony Care) - Turquoise
- C+ (Riding) - Burgundy
- C+ both sections - Pink
- B (Riding) - Beige
- B (Horse & Pony Care) - Brown
- B both sections - Red
- Lungeing test - Light Blue
- B+ - Pale Purple
- AH - Orange
- AH with Distinction - Orange
- AH with Honours - Salmon Pink
- A - Blue
- A with Distinction - Blue
- A with Honours - Purple

Reasonable Adjustments

The Pony Club is committed to ensuring that, wherever possible, members are able to access all aspects of the Branch and Centre activities we offer. Reasonable Adjustments are any actions that help to reduce the effect of a disability or difficulty. They are needed because some disabilities can make it harder for members to take part in activities than it would have been had the member not been disabled. A Member does not necessarily have to be disabled (as defined by the Equality Act 2010) to be allowed an access arrangement. Reasonable adjustments are intended to increase access to Tests and other activities and are intended to assist Members in demonstrating their attainment without affecting or circumventing the Test requirements. All Reasonable Adjustment Plans will be treated confidentially and only shared with permission from the member and their parent (if under 18yrs old).

Reasonable Adjustments can be used for th Pony Club Tests and should be approved in advance of the Test taking place. Reasonabl adjustments are changes made to an assessment or to the way an assessment is conducted that reduce or remove a disadvantage caused by a student's disabilit Reasonable Adjustments will not affect the reliability or validity of the Test outcome nor should they give the Member an assessmen advantage over other Members undertakin the same or similar Tests. Where possible the reasonable adjustment should reflect a Member's normal way of working. The Reasonable Adjustment is intended to give all Pony Club Members a level playing field i which to demonstrate their skills, knowledg and understanding.

Reasonable Adjustments can also be used t allow for members to take part in activities c competitions. As with Tests these adjustmen should be approved in advance of the activi or competition.

Some Pony Club members may already have an Education, Health and Care Plan (EHCP) which can be used to help plan Reasonable Adjustments. However, the Pony Club will strive to ensure inclusivity for any of its members who need additional support whether or not they have an official statement.

PONY CLUB ACTIVITIES

WORKING RALLIES

The working rally continues to be an important part of Pony Club training with the main objectives being to encourage and improve members' riding skills and their knowledge of equine care and management.

Rallies must be advertised at least seven days prior to the date of the rally and organised by Branch / Centre Committees. Nobody can hold a rally or coach at a rally unless authorised by the District Commissioner, Branch Committee or Centre Proprietor.

A working rally is one at which coaching is given and which is open to all members of the Branch / Centre within the age range or ability level for which it is intended, it may be mounted or dismounted. A dismounted rally is usually used for horse and pony care instruction. Team practices or coaching sessions limited those members selected for a team do not qualify as working rallies (discretion may be used in cases where members are working or in further education).

The Pony Club syllabus of coaching in The Pony Club Instructors' Handbook offers guidance on how to build a programme. The timetable and the coaching given at Rallies should be carefully planned.

UNSUITABLE HORSES/PONIES AND UNSUITABLE SADDLERY

Members may come to mounted rallies on horses/ponies which are unsuitable for them or with ill-fitting saddlery that is unserviceable. This can make instruction difficult and the safety of both rider and horse/pony must take precedence. Members coming to a rally for the first time who may not know of The Pony Club's standards and training ethos which will need addressing with tact and sympathy and offered in the form of education and encouragement.

At the start of every working rally the coach should observe riders to ensure the correct gear is worn, and check on the fitting of tack, giving appropriate advice. Where there is a problem, which makes riding impossible, or dangerous, the rider should be asked to dismount and the problem passed to The Pony Club official in charge of the rally. If there is need to involve the member's parents this should be done by the District Commissioner/ Centre Proprietor or the Rally Organiser. Action by the coach is not recommended.

COMPETITIONS

Open Horse Shows and Competitions

To raise funds some Branches and Centres organise shows or competitions that are open to non- Members.

A disclaimer should be included in the programme for all shows and competitions organised by Branches/Centres. The suggested wording is:

> **"Legal Liability: Save for the death or personal injury caused by the negligence of the organisers, or anyone for whom they are in law responsible, neither the organisers of this event or The Pony Club nor any agent, employee or representative of these bodies, nor the landlord or his tenant, accepts any liability for any accident, loss, damage, injury or illness to horses, owners, riders, spectators, land, cars, their contents and accessories, or any other person or property whatsoever. Entries are only accepted on this basis.**
>
> **Health & Safety: Organisers of this event have taken reasonable precautions to ensure the health and safety of everyone present. For these measures to be effective,**

everyone must take all reasonable precautions to avoid and prevent accidents occurring and must obey the instructions of the organisers and all the officials and stewards.

Competitors who are not members of The Pony Club are not covered by The Pony Club insurance and must have their own third party cover. The [XX] Branch of The Pony Club/[xx} Pony Club Centre and the organisers of this event are not legally responsible for non-Members and their insurance will not cover you."

When holding classes for which conditions have been laid down, and judges appointed by a governing body, Branches and Centres are recommended to seek advice from the organisation concerned.

Prizes

It is against Pony Club policy to encourage children to be 'pot hunters' and money prizes are forbidden at competitions or shows for Pony Club Members only.

Competitions Open to Members of other Branches or Centres

Members and organisers of events must follow the Rule for Competitions organised by Branches and Centres.

If an event is open to competitors from other Branches or Centres, it is important to put in the schedule under which Rules it is run and any local modifications.

Types Of Competition

Dismounted

- National Quiz
- Horse & Pony Care Competition
- Triathlon

Mounted

- Dressage
- Dressage to Music
- Endurance
- Equitation Dressage and Show Jumping
- Eventing (including Arena Eventing)
- Hunter Trials
- Mounted Games
- Musical Ride
- Pony Racing
- Polo
- Polocrosse
- Show Jumping
- Tetrathlon

DRESSAGE TESTS

Level	Area	Championship
Regional Championships	Grassroots Dressage Test 2018	Grassroots Dressage Test 2018
Novice	Novice Dressage Test 2020	Novice Dressage Championship Test 2017
Intermediate	**Intermediate Dressage Test 2022**	Intermediate Dressage Championship Test 2014
Open	Open Dressage Test 2020	Open Dressage Championship Test 2018

EVENTING TESTS

Level	Area	Championship
Regional Championships	Grassroots Dressage Test 2018	Grassroots Dressage Test 2018
PC90	PC90 Eventing Test 2013	PC90 Eventing Championship Test 2015

PC100	PC100 Eventing Test 2015	PC100 Eventing Championship Test 2013
PC100+	**PC110 Eventing Test 2022**	PC110 Eventing Championship Test 2015
PC110	**PC110 Eventing Test 2022**	PC110 Eventing Championship Test 2015

DRESSAGE JUDGES

It is recommended that for all Dressage Tests, a Judge from British Dressage's Official Judges Panel is used so that the guidance given to Members is of a high standard. The required list of Judge can be found in the Pony Club Dressage Rule Book.

The British Dressage Judges Panel can be found on the BD website: britishdressage.co.uk

HUNTING

The Pony Club and its Branches are entirely separate organisations to any hunts. Historically Branches were founded by members of local Hunts for the benefit of their farmers' and subscribers' children.

The Pony Club recognises that hunting has changed following the inception of the Hunting Act 2004 on 18th February 2005. As long as hunts are acting within the law, The Pony Club continues to encourage those Members who wish to take part and experience riding across country to do so.

Trail-hunting, hound exercise and exempt hunting are recognised activities that hunts participate in to comply with the current legislation.

EXCHANGES BETWEEN BRANCHES, CENTRES AND INTERNATIONAL VISITS

The Pony Club believes that visits and the exchange of ideas between Branches and Centres offers a great benefit to Members. The sharing of interests with Members from different Branches and Centres and from different countries broadens a Member's experience.

Areas, Branches or Centres wanting to arrange exchanges or visits, where they will be representing The Pony Club, with countries or overseas Branches or Centres must first get permission from The Pony Club Office and their Area Representative. Details of these visits must be sent to The Pony Club Office and their Area Representative who will give guidance and support where possible. At the end of any visit, a written report will be required by The Pony Club Office.

For an exchange that relates to a specific sport please take note of the selection criteria which apply to that sport, available on The Pony Club website.

All International invitations are made direct to The Pony Club Office in conjunction with the Pony Club International Alliance (PCIA).

YOUTH PROGRAMMES

Young Equestrian Leader Award (YELA)

The Young Equestrian Leaders Award is a scheme which recognises the time and effort that young people put in to volunteering in equestrian sport. It is open to Pony Club Members aged between 13 and 25 with three levels available: Bronze, Silver and Gold. The progressive requirements at each level encourage young people to develop a range of skills, gain experiences and learn more about the industry in view of shaping them to become leaders of the future.

Once registered, young people will be sent a log book to track and record their volunteering, with just 20 hours gaining them the Bronze level. For more information please visit The Pony Club website or email yela@pcuk.org

Schools

The Pony Club is developing a programme joins primary schools up to their local Pony Club Linked Riding Centre to give young people a taster of horse riding and what the sport involves.

Thanks to funding from Sport England and support from British Equestrian, the project offers primary schools around the country access to classroom sessions suitable for classes or whole year groups in years 3-5. These sessions engage students through a variety of fun and creative exercises, whilst introducing the basics of pony welfare. The second stage of the project involves linking the primary school to their local Pony Club Linked Riding Centre so that students can meet the ponies and practically learn about riding and caring for them. All students receive a Pony Club workbook as well as a discount off their first riding lesson should they wish to visit the Pony Club Centre in future.

THE PONY CLUB WEBSITE

Aim

The purpose of The Pony Club Website is to provide a source of information, education and interactive activities for all. It can be found at pcuk.org.

The Branch And Area Sites

All Branches and Areas have their own sub-site which can be accessed and updated. These websites can be found through the "Find a Club" listings on pcuk.org

The District Commissioner should call for a volunteer to take on the responsibility of acting as Web Manager and managing the Branch site. Each Branch is responsible for writing and updating its own Branch pages and must have access to a computer, which can connect to the Internet, in order to do this. Each site can have multiple managers required. The Pony Club will never ask you fo your password.

THE PONY CLUB EMAIL SYSTEM

All Branches and Areas have their own emai address ending in @pcuk.org to which all official communications will be sent. At leas one member of the Branch committee mus have access to this email account and the District Commissioner should ensure that it checked regularly.

Emails can be accessed through a webmail interface, by using software such as Microso Outlook or by adding to a phone or tablet. Access details and further information can b requested by contacting The Pony Club Offi or the PELHAM Support hub: https://pelham pcuk.org

Passwords should be changed frequently and kept secure. If responsibility for the ema system passes to another volunteer the password should be changed to maintain a high level of security.

THE PELHAM SYSTEM

This system keeps a list of all current and pas Members for each Branch or Centre along with information on Branch/Centre Officials and Coaches. All new Members and renewir Members are processed via The Pony Club Office for both Branch and Centres.

All Branches are required to keep the contac information up-to-date on a regular basis to satisfy both insurance requirements and Da Protection legislation. Branches should also record Tests and Achievement Badges on this system.

Branches should also maintain up-to-date coach information, including Disclosure, Safeguarding, First Aid and CPD certifications on PELHAM.

Centres - please regularly check your Membership records. Centres can also record Tests and Achievement Badges on this system. Coach data for Centres will be updated by Centre Co-ordinators or The Pony Club Office.

In additional to holding data, the PELHAM system also provides email facility for members and coaches, transfer of Members.

You do not require any special software to access PELHAM; you just need a computer with internet access. Please check the PELHAM support site for user guides and up-to-date information: https://pelham.pcuk.org

TRAVELLING EXPENSES

In accordance with Rule 12.5, the currently approved rate when travelling by car is 45 pence per mile for the first 10,000 miles, and 25 pence per mile for any subsequent mileage.

Pony Club Areas

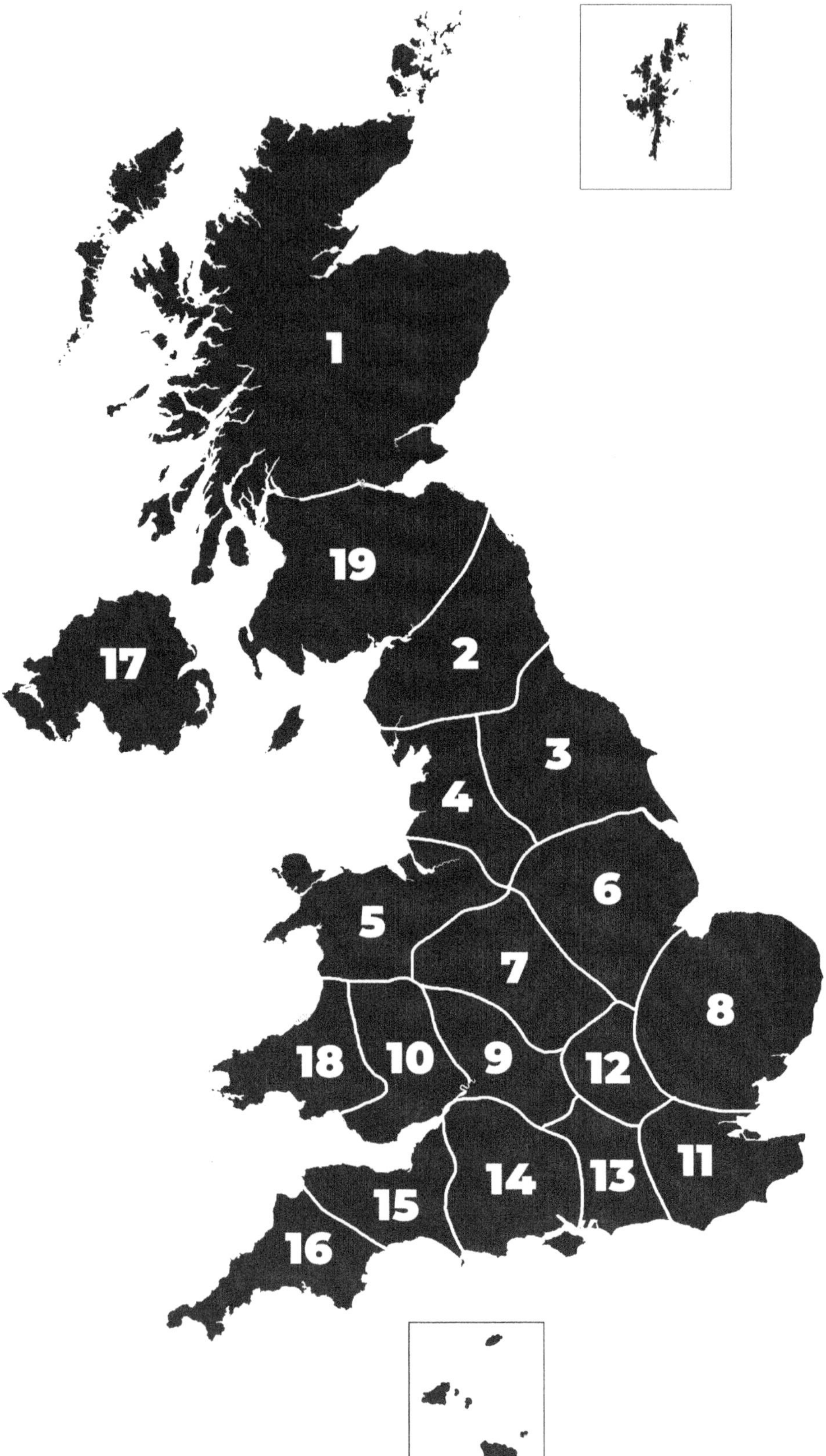

AREA 1

Area Representative: Catriona Willison

area1@pcuk.org
01360 860257 / 07979 735274

Centre Coordinator: Adrian Macleod

area1.centres@pcuk.org
07866 631875

BRANCHES

- Aberdeenshire
- Angus
- Bennachie
- Caithness
- Deeside
- Deveron
- East Aberdeenshire (Buchan)
- East Stirlingshire
- Fife Hunt
- Forth Valley
- Glenrothes
- Inverness-shire
- Kincardineshire
- Moray & Nairn
- North Argyll
- Orkney
- Perth Hunt
- Ross-shire
- Strathearn
- West Perthshire
- Western Isles

CENTRES

- Achalone Activities
- Broom Farm Riding
- Broomhill Riding Centre
- Cabin Equestrian Centre
- Castle View Stables
- Dark Deer Croft
- Glen Tanar Equestrian Centre
- Gleneagles Equestrian Centre
- Hayfield EC
- Horsin Around
- Pathhead Equestrian Centre
- Scholland Equestrian at Kilconquhar
- Skye Trekking Centre
- Tannoch Stables
- The Leys Riding School (prev. Sea Horse Stables)
- Uist Community Riding School
- Wardhaugh Farm
- Wellsfield Equestrian Centre
- Wester Dowald Equine Centre

AREA 2

Area Representative: Sheila Clifford

area2@pcuk.org
0191 388 3756

Centre Coordinator: Sarah Lewins

area2.centres@pcuk.org
07799 404246

BRANCHES

- Braes of Derwent South
- Cleveland Hunt
- Cumberland Farmers' Hunt (South)
- Cumberland Farmers Hunt North
- Cumberland Foxhounds
- East Cleveland
- Morpeth Hunt
- Newcastle & North Durham
- North Northumberland Hunt
- Percy Hunt
- South Durham Hunt
- South Northumberland
- Tynedale Hunt
- West Cumberland
- Wyndham
- Zetland Hunt

CENTRES

- Bank House Equestrian
- Blackdyke Farm Riding and Competition Centre
- Calvert Trust Pony Club Centre
- Eston Equitation Centre
- Field House Equestrian Centre
- Finchale View Riding School
- Fir Tree Farm Equestrian Centre Ltd
- Murton Equestrian Centre
- Robinsons Equiteach

- Rookin House Farm
- Stainsby Grange Equestrian Centre
- Swinhoe Farm Riding Centre
- The Unicorn Centre

AREA 3

Area Representative: Nicky Morrison
area3@pcuk.org
01677 450998

Centre Coordinator: Emily Massey
area3.centres@pcuk.org
07826 430047

BRANCHES

- Badsworth Hunt
- Bedale & West of Yore Hunt
- Bramham Moor Hunt
- Derwent Hunt
- Glaisdale Hunt
- Goathland Hunt
- Holderness Hunt
- Hurworth Hunt
- Middleton Hunt
- Middleton Hunt (East Side)
- Rockwood Harriers
- Ryburn Valley
- Sinnington Hunt
- Staintondale Hunt
- Vale of York
- York & Ainsty North
- York & Ainsty South

CENTRES

- Acre Cliffe Equestrian Centre
- Angel Riding Centre
- Batley Hall Farm Riding Centre
- Bewerley Riding Centre
- Bridge End Equestrian
- Burnby Equestrian Centre
- Cliffhollins Riding School
- Friars Hill Stables
- Grenoside Equestrian Centre Ltd
- Lime Oaks Equestrian Centre
- Meadow View Stables
- Middleton Park Equestrian Centre
- Naburn Grange Riding Centre
- Nether Hall Riding School
- Oxmardyke Equestrian Centre
- Riverside Equestrian Centre
- Throstle Nest Riding School
- Tong Lane End Equestrian Centre
- Vale Mill Pony Club Centre
- Yorkshire Riding Centre

AREA 4

Area Representative: Robin Bower
area4@pcuk.org
07976 272272

Centre Coordinator: John Gilbert
area4.centres@pcuk.org
07837 597561

BRANCHES

- Blackburn & District
- Chipping
- Furness & District
- Fylde & District
- Glossop & District
- Haydock Park
- Holcombe Hunt
- Isle of Man
- Lancaster & District
- Oxenholme
- Peak
- Pendle Forest & Craven Hunt
- Saddleworth & District
- West Lancashire County
- West Lancashire Ince Blundell
- Wheelton & District

CENTRES

- Accrington Riding Centre
- Ballawhetstone
- Beaumont Grange Farm
- Bigland Hall Equine Group
- Bold Heath Equestrian Centre
- Bowlers Riding School
- Burrows Lane Farm Riding School
- Casterton Sedbergh Prep School
- Croft Riding Centre Pony Club

- Dam Top Riding Centre
- Darlington Stables
- Deandane Riding Stables
- Eccleston Equestrian Centre
- Grenaby Estates Limited
- Hargate Hill Equestrian Centre
- Holt's Equestrian Centre
- Kilnsey Trekking and Riding Centre
- Landlords Farm Equestrian Centre
- Larkrigg Riding School
- Lodge Riding Centre
- Longfield Equestrian Centre
- Manchester Pony Club Centre
- Midgeland Riding School
- Moorview Equestrian Centre
- New Hill House
- Robin House Equestrian
- Roocroft Riding Stables
- Seaview Riding School
- Simonswood Riding Academy
- Witherslack Hall Equestrian Centre
- Wrea Green Equitation Centre

AREA 5

Area Representative: Andrew Tulloch
area5@pcuk.org
07831 315104

Centre Coordinator: John Gilbert
area5.centres@pcuk.org
07837 597561

BRANCHES

- Aberconwy
- Anglesey
- Berwyn & Dee
- Burton Cheshire Forest Hunt
- Cheshire Hunt North
- Cheshire Hunt South
- Dolgellau & District
- Dwyfor
- East Cheshire
- Flint & Denbigh Hunt
- Gwynedd
- Sir W W Wynn's Hunt
- Tanatside Hunt
- Waen-y-Llyn

CENTRES

- Bridlewood Riding Centre
- Cheshire Riding School
- Coleg Cambria
- Conwy Community Riding Centre
- Daisy Bank Farm
- Gorswen Riding School
- Llannerch Equestrian Centre
- Oakhanger Riding and Pony Club Centre
- Pen Y Coed Riding Stables
- Raby House Stables
- Snowdonia Riding Stables
- Springbank Riding School
- Springhill Farm Riding Stables
- Willington Hall Riding Centre
- Wirral Riding Centre

AREA 6

Area Representative: Patrick Campbell
area6@pcuk.org
07801 423898

Centre Coordinator: Amelia Morris-Payne
area6.centres@pcuk.org
07816 955757

BRANCHES

- Barlow Hunt
- Belvoir Hunt
- Blankney Hunt
- Brocklesby Hunt
- Burghley
- Burton Hunt
- Cottesmore Hunt
- Fernie Hunt
- Fitzwilliam Hunt
- Grove Hunt
- High Peak Hunt
- Meynell Hunt
- Quorn Hunt
- Rufford Hunt
- Scunthorpe & District
- South Nottinghamshire
- South Trent
- South Wold Hunt North
- Woodland Pytchley Hunt

CENTRES

- Almond Equestrian
- Brackenside Stables
- Brimington Equestrian Centre
- Brooksby Equestrian Centre
- Bulby Hall Equestrian Centre
- Caistor Equestrian Centre
- Chestnut Farm Stables
- Coloured Cob Equestrian Centre
- Cottagers Plot Equestrian Centre
- Dovecote Farm Equestrian Centre
- Folly Farm Equestrian Centre
- Four Winds Equestrian Centre
- Grove House Stables Pony Club Centre
- Hargate Equestrian
- Hill House School Pony Club
- Hundleby Riding Centre
- Knowle Hill Equestrian
- Langtoft Stables
- Long Lane Equestrian
- Meadow School of Riding
- Mere Lane Equestrian Centre
- Mill House
- Newark Equestrian
- Oakfield Farm Pony Club Centre
- Oldmoor Farm Riding School
- Orchard Farm Equestrian Centre
- P and R Equestrian Centre
- Parklands Arena
- Parkside Stables
- Parkview Riding School
- Poppyfield Equestrian
- Red Piece Equestrian Stables
- Ringer Villa Farm
- Scropton Riding and Driving Centre
- Snowdon Farm Riding School
- Somerby Equestrian Centre
- Southview Equestrian Centre
- Stickney Riding Centre

AREA 7

Area Representative: Andrew James
area7@pcuk.org
01455 291273 / 07737 877697

Centre Coordinator: Karen Hudson
area7.centres@pcuk.org
07974 182664

BRANCHES

- Albrighton Hunt
- Albrighton Woodland Hunt
- Atherstone Hunt
- Heart of England
- Ludlow Hunt
- North Shropshire Hunt
- North Staffordshire Hunt
- North Warwickshire
- Pytchley Hunt
- South Shropshire Hunt
- South Staffordshire Hunt
- United Pack
- Warwickshire Hunt
- West Midlands
- West Warwickshire
- Wheatland Hunt

CENTRES

- Abbotsholme Equestrian Centre
- Appletree Stud
- Beaver Hall
- Bishton Hall Riding School
- Bourne Vale Riding Stables
- Brampton Stables
- Corner Farm Equestrian
- Coton House Farm Stables
- Country Treks
- Courses for Horses
- Coventry and District Pony Club
- East Lodge Farm Equestrian Centre
- Equine Learning
- Featherbed Stables
- Foxhills Riding Centre
- Grafton Farm Riding Centre Ltd
- Highcross Equestrian Centre

- Hole Farm Trekking Centre
- K A Horses
- Lodge Farm Equestrian Centre
- Lychgate Farm Equestrian LLP
- Moor Farm Stables
- Mousley House Farm Equestrian Centre
- Nuneaton and North Warwickshire Equestrian Centre
- Radway Riding School LLP
- Rockstar Equine
- Rookery Team Pony Club
- Stourport Riding Centre
- Summerfield Stables
- Valley Farm Equestrian Centre Ltd
- Witham Villa Riding Centre
- Woodbine Stables

AREA 8

Area Representative: Hetta Wilkinson

area8@pcuk.org
07880 728708 / 01206 330476

Centre Coordinator: Di Pegrum

area8.centres@pcuk.org
07890 919558

BRANCHES

- Cambridgeshire Hunt
- East Essex Hunt
- Easton Harriers Hunt
- Enfield Chace Hunt
- Essex & Suffolk Hunt
- Essex Farmers
- Essex Hunt North
- Essex Union
- Essex Union South
- Littleport & District
- Newmarket & Thurlow Hunt
- North Norfolk
- Puckeridge Hunt
- Puckeridge Hunt Western
- Soham & District
- South Norfolk
- Suffolk Hunt
- Thetford Chase
- Walpole & District
- Waveney Harriers
- West Norfolk Hunt

CENTRES

- Aldborough Hall Equestrian Centre
- Annabelles Equestrian
- Apollo Stables
- Barnfields (8) Riding School
- Brook Cottage Farm Riding School
- Deanswood Equestrian Centre
- Fletchers Farm Riding School
- Gillians Riding School Pony Club Centre
- Gym-Khana Club at Valley Farm
- Hall Farm Stables
- Hill Farm Equestrian Centre (8)
- Hill Farm Stables and Livery Yard
- Hilltop Equestrian Centre
- Hooks Cross Equestrian
- Hot to Trot School of Equitation
- Iken Bay Riding
- Kimblewick Equestrian Centre
- Lee Valley Riding Centre
- Little Wratting Riding School
- Moat Farm Riding Centre
- Moor Hall Farm Polo Centre
- North Manor Equestrian Centre
- Northbrook Equestrian Centre
- Old Tiger Stables
- Park Hall Equestrian
- Petasfield Stables
- Poplar Park Equestrian Centre
- Roman Bank Equestrian
- Running Well Equestrian Centre
- Sawston Riding School
- The Pony Ranch
- Trent Park Equestrian Centre
- Willow Farm Riding School
- Withersfield Hall Equestrian Centre

AREA 9

Area Representative: Pleasance Jewitt
area9@pcuk.org
01285 821715

Centre Coordinator: Lea Allen
area9.centres@pcuk.org
07801 278785

BRANCHES

- Beaufort Hunt
- Berkeley Hunt
- Berkeley Hunt South
- Cotswold Hunt
- Cotswold Vale Farmers' Hunt
- Croome Hunt
- Heythrop Hunt
- Ledbury Hunt
- Malvern
- Minchinhampton
- North Cotswold Hunt
- North Herefordshire Hunt
- Old Berkshire Hunt
- South Hereford and Ross Harriers
- Stroud
- VWH Hunt
- Worcestershire Hunt
- Wyre Forest

CENTRES

- Asti Equestrian
- Bourton Vale Equestrian Centre
- Cotswold Riding
- Defence Academy Saddle Club
- Foxcote House Riding School
- Huntersfield Equestrian Centre
- Malvern Riding School
- Noakes Farm Riding Centre
- Pigeon House Equestrian
- Putley Pony Club Centre
- Regal Equestrian
- St James City Farm and Riding School
- Tewkesbury Pony Club Centre
- The Elms
- The Talland School of Equitation
- Tipton Hall Riding School
- Tumpy Green Equestrian & Competition Centre
- Wickstead Farm Equestrian Centre
- Worcester Riding School and Pony Club Centre

AREA 10

Area Representative: Isobel Mills
area10@pcuk.org
07976 779140

Centre Coordinator: Lea Allen
area10.centres@pcuk.org
07801 278785

BRANCHES

- Brecon & Talybont Hunt
- Crickhowell & District
- Curre Hunt
- Dare Valley
- Dinas Powys
- Glamorgan Hunt
- Golden Valley Hunt
- Irfon & Tywi
- Kenfig Hill
- Llangeinor Hunt
- Llangibby Hunt
- Monmouthshire
- Pentyrch
- Radnor & West Hereford Hunt
- Sennybridge & District
- Teme Valley Hunt
- Tredegar Farmers Hunt
- Ynysybwl

CENTRES

- Cantref Pony Club Centre
- Cardiff Riding School
- Green Meadow Riding Centre
- Liege Manor Equestrian
- Lucton School
- Severnvale Equestrian Centre
- Smugglers Equestrian Centre
- Sunnybank Equestrian Centre
- Talygarn Equestrian Centre
- Tregoyd Riding Centre

- Triley Fields Equestrian Centre
- Underhill Riding Stables

AREA 11

Area Representative: Abby Bernard
area11@pcuk.org
07775 712512

Centre Coordinator: Sarah Glynn-Brooks
area11.centres@pcuk.org
07816 784487

BRANCHES

- Ashford Valley Hunt
- Cobham and Wimbledon
- Crawley & Horsham Hunt
- East Kent Hunt
- East Sussex
- Eridge Hunt
- Isle of Sheppey
- Kent Border
- Mid Surrey
- North West Kent
- Old Surrey & Burstow Hunt
- Romney Marsh
- Southdown Hunt (East)
- Southdown Hunt West
- Surrey Union
- Tickham Hunt
- West Kent (Sevenoaks)
- West Kent Meopham

CENTRES

- Ashdown Forest Riding Centre
- Barton Field Farm Equestrian Centre
- Bradbourne Riding and Training Centre
- Braeside Equestrian Centre Area11
- Buckswood School Stables
- Bursted Manor Riding Centre
- Cornilo Riding
- Cuckoo Riding Centre
- Deen City Farm
- Deepdene Riding Stables
- Ebony Horse Club
- Ghyll Park Equestrian
- Grove Farm Riding School
- Hemsted Forest Equestrian Centre
- Horseshoes Riding School
- Kent College Equine Unit
- Kingsmead Equestrian Centre
- Kingston Riding Centre
- Lancing Equestrian
- Little Brook Equestrian
- Lower Farm Stables
- Mierscourt Valley Riding School
- Mount Mascal Stables
- Nelson Park Riding Centre
- Nightingale Farm and Stud
- Old Bexley Stables Pony Club
- Park Farm Riding School
- Park Lane Stables
- Pine Ridge Riding School
- Quarry Farm Riding Stables
- Ridge Farm Riding School
- Royal Alexandra and Albert School RS
- Rye Street Farm Equestrian Centre
- Saddles Riding Centre
- South Farm Riding Stables
- Southborough Lane Stables
- Squirrells Riding School
- St Teresa's Equestrian
- Stag Lodge
- Tandridge Priory Riding Centre
- The 4 Gaits Riding School
- The Owl House Stables
- The Stables at Cissbury
- Timbertops Equestrian Centre
- Trenley Park Liveries
- Valley Riding School
- Wellgrove Farm Equestrian
- Whiteleaf Riding Stables
- Wildwoods Riding Centre

AREA 12

Area Representative: Helen Jackson
area12@pcuk.org
01494 881321 / 07941 818738

Centre Coordinator: Di Pegrum
area12.centres@pcuk.org
07890 919558

BRANCHES

- Bedfordshire South
- Bicester & Warden Hill Hunt
- East Hertfordshire Hunt
- Flamstead
- Grafton Hunt
- Hertfordshire Hunt
- Ivel Valley
- Oakley Hunt North
- Oakley Hunt West
- Old Berkeley Hunt (Chilterns)
- Old Berkeley Hunt (Hughenden)
- Old Berkeley Hunt (North)
- Old Berkeley Hunt (South)
- South Hertfordshire
- South Oxfordshire Hunt (South)
- South Oxfordshire Hunt Central
- Vale of Aylesbury Hunt
- Whaddon Chase
- Woodland Hunt
- Wormwood Scrubs

CENTRES

- Baylands Equestrian Centre
- Blisworth Pony Club Centre
- Brook Stables
- Bryerley Springs Equestrian Centre
- Ealing Riding School
- Echos Equestrian
- Evergreen Stables
- Goulds Green Riding School
- Littlebourne Equestrian Centre
- Sandridgebury Riding School
- Shardeloes Farm Equestrian Centre
- Silverstone Riding Stables
- Snowball Farm Equestrian Centre
- Waterstock Dressage Ltd
- Widmer Equestrian

AREA 13

Area Representative: Sara Tremlett
area13@pcuk.org
01798 813543 / 07831 695311

Centre Coordinator: Sally Blackmore
area13.centres@pcuk.org
07442 530080

BRANCHES

- Bisley and Sandown Chase
- Chiddingfold
- Chiddingfold Farmers
- Cowdray Hunt
- Crawley & Horsham Hunt South
- Garth Hunt
- Garth South
- Goodwood
- Hambledon Hunt (North)
- Hampshire Hunt
- Isle of Wight
- Lord Leconfield Hunt
- Petersfield
- South Berkshire
- Staff College & Sandhurst
- Vine
- Wokingham

CENTRES

- Badshot Lea Equestrian Centre
- Barnfield Riding School
- Berkshire Riding Centre
- Broadlands Riding Centre
- Catherington Equestrian Centre
- Cranleigh School Equestrian Centre
- Equestrian at Coworth Park
- Fort Widley Equestrian Centre
- Gleneagles Equestrian Centre (Area 13)
- Greatham Equestrian Centre
- Greenways Stables Ltd
- Hewshott Farm Stables
- Hill Farm Riding Stables and Pony Club Centre (IoW)

- Hollyoaks Riding
- Inadown Farm Livery Stables
- Island Riding Centre
- Kiln Stables Riding School
- Lands End Equestrian Centre
- Lavant Equestrian
- Northington Stud and Stables
- Pony Grove
- Quob Stables Equestrian Centre
- Russells Equestrian Centre
- Shedfield Equestrian Centre
- Silvermere Equestrian Centre
- Wellington Riding

AREA 14

Area Representative: Louly Thornycroft
area14@pcuk.org
01258 860614

Centre Coordinator: Sara Greenwood
area14.centres@pcuk.org
07773 782052

BRANCHES

- Avon Vale Hunt
- Banwell
- Blackmore & Sparkford Vale Hunt
- Cattistock Hunt
- Craven Hunt
- Guernsey
- Hursley Hunt
- Jersey Drag Hunt
- Mendip Farmers' Hunt
- New Forest Hunts
- Poole & District
- Portman Hunt
- Royal Artillery
- South & West Wilts Hunt
- South Dorset Hunt
- Syston
- Tedworth Hunt
- West Hants
- Wilton Hunt
- Wylye Valley

CENTRES

- Alstone Court Riding Establishment
- Burley Villa School of Riding
- Church Farm Equestrian Centre
- Ebborlands Riding Centre
- Hanford School
- Kingston Maurward College
- Knighton House School
- Otterbourne Riding Centre
- Pevlings Farm Riding and Livery Stables
- Rosewall Equestrian
- Royal Armoured Corps Saddle Club
- Sandroyd School
- SMS Equestrian
- Stonar School Equestrian Centre
- Tedworth Equestrian
- Wick Riding School
- Widbrook Arabian Stud and Equestrian Centre

AREA 15

**Area Representative:
Deborah Custance-Baker**
area15@pcuk.org
01392 861750 / 07889 260446

Centre Coordinator: Vacant
area15.centres@pcuk.org

BRANCHES

- Axe Vale Hunt
- Cotley Hunt
- Devon & Somerset
- Dulverton West Foxhounds (North Molton) Hunt
- East Devon Hunt
- Polden Hills
- Quantock Hunt
- Seavington
- Silverton Hunt
- Taunton Vale
- Taunton Vale Harriers
- Tiverton Hunt
- West Somerset
- Weston Harriers Hunt

CENTRES

- Bowdens Riding School at Balham
- Comeytrowe Equestrian Centre
- Currypool Equestrian
- Drakes Farm Riding School
- Mutterton Equine
- Oaklands Riding School (Area 15)
- QSR Equestrian Centre
- Red Park Equestrian Centre
- Woolacombe Riding Stables

AREA 16

Area Representative: Karen Harris
area16@pcuk.org

Centre Coordinator: Helen Moore
area16.centres@pcuk.org
07828 837784

BRANCHES

- Cury Hunt
- Dartmoor Hunt
- East Cornwall Hunt
- Eggesford Hunt
- Four Burrow Hunt
- Lamerton Hunt
- Mid Devon Hunt
- North Cornwall
- South Devon Hunt (Moorland)
- South Devon West
- South Pool
- Spooners & West Dartmoor
- Stevenstone & Torrington Farmers Hunt
- Tetcott & South Tetcott Hunts
- Western Hunt

CENTRES

- Barguse Riding Centre
- Coker Brown School of Riding
- Hunterswood Riding and Livery Stables
- La Rocco Riding School
- Lakefield Equestrian Centre
- Lauras Lessons
- Little Margate Equestrian
- Lower Tokenbury Equestrian Centre
- Newton Equestrian
- Newton Ferrers Equus
- St Leonards Equitation Centre

AREA 17

Area Representative: Liz Lowry
area17@pcuk.org
02891 870766

Centre Coordinator: Vacant
area17.centres@pcuk.org

BRANCHES

- East Antrim
- East Down
- Fermanagh Harriers
- Iveagh
- Killultagh Old Rock & Chichester Harriers
- Mid Antrim
- North Derry
- North Down
- Route Hunt
- Seskinore Harriers
- Tullylagan

CENTRES

- Birr House Riding Centre
- City of Derry Equestrian Centre
- Faughanvale Stables
- Free Spirit Equestrian
- Galgorm Parks Riding School
- Island Magee Riding Centre
- Kays Equestrian
- Laurel View Equestrian Centre
- Lodge Equine Stables
- RD Equestrian
- St Patricks Way Stables
- Tullymurray Equestrian Centre

AREA 18

Area Representative: Julie Hodson
area18@pcuk.org
01239 654314

Centre Coordinator: Lea Allen
area18.centres@pcuk.org
07801 278785

BRANCHES

- Amman Valley & District
- Banwen & District
- Carmarthen Bay
- Gogerddan
- Llandeilo & District
- Neath
- Parc Howard
- Pembrokeshire Hunt
- Rheidol Riding Centre
- South Pembrokeshire & Cresselly Hunt
- St Davids & District
- Swansea & District
- Tivyside
- Vale of Clettwr
- Vale of Taf

CENTRES

- Bowlings Riding School
- Cefngranod Stables
- Cimla Trekking and Equestrian Centre
- Clyne Farm Centre
- Dinefwr Riding Centre
- Green Farm Riding Stables
- Havard Stables
- Marros Riding Centre
- Priory Stables

AREA 19

Area Representative: Anne Ekin
area19@pcuk.org
07711 630433

Centre Coordinator: Lea Allen
area19.centres@pcuk.org
07801 278785

BRANCHES

- Argyll South
- Berwickshire Hunt
- Dalkeith & District
- Duke of Buccleuch's Hunt
- Dumfriesshire Hunt
- East Lothian
- Edinburgh
- Eglinton Hunt
- Eskdale
- Galloway
- Isle of Mull
- Lanark & Upperward
- Lanarkshire & Renfrewshire Hunt
- Lauderdale Hunt
- Linlithgow & Stirlingshire
- Nithsdale
- Peebles Tweeddale
- Stewartry
- Strathblane & District

CENTRES

- Argyll Adventure
- Fergushill Riding Stables
- Fordbank Equi Centre
- Wardhouse Equestrian Centre

PONY CLUB BRANCHES IN THE UK

Founding Branches are denoted by a sideline next to their name

Aberconwy (1974)
Area 5
aberconwy@pcuk.org
DC Jessica Foulkes-Kelly
Sec Gwawr Williams

Aberdeenshire (1931)
Area 1
aberdeenshire@pcuk.org
DC Pamela Charles
Sec Claire Cochran

Albrighton Hunt (1933)
Area 7
albrighton@pcuk.org
DC Rory Howard
Sec Helen Howard

Albrighton Woodland Hunt (1932)
Area 7
albrightonwoodland@pcuk.org
DC Trevor Brighton
Sec Kim Murrells

Amman Valley & District (1966)
Area 18
ammanvalley@pcuk.org
DC Elizabeth Ivey
Sec Sue James

Anglesey (1984)
Area 5
anglesey@pcuk.org
DC Jill Owen
Sec Louise Richardson

Angus (1949)
Area 1
angus@pcuk.org
DC Kirsty Geddes
Sec Tricia Hynd

Argyll South (1980)
Area 19
argyllsouth@pcuk.org
DC Lucia Boase
Sec Elizabeth MacNab

Ashford Valley Hunt (1934)
Area 11
ashfordvalley@pcuk.org
DC Philippa Jones
Sec Samantha Parsler

Atherstone Hunt (1931)
Area 7
atherstone@pcuk.org
DC Emma Neal
Sec Charlotte Mawdesley

Avon Vale Hunt (1947)
Area 14
avonvale@pcuk.org
DC Katharine McNamara
DC Haylely Cole
Sec Sarah Bentley

Axe Vale Hunt (1958)
Area 15
axevale@pcuk.org
DC Danielle Jones

Badsworth Hunt (1930)
Area 3
badsworth@pcuk.org
DC Charlie Warde-Aldam
Sec Wendy Truelove

Banwell (1960)
Area 14
banwell@pcuk.org
DC Imogen Rogers-Nash
Sec Verity Wring

Banwen & District (1956)
Area 18
banwen@pcuk.org
DC Chris Powell
Sec Dennis Whitney

Barlow Hunt (1934)
Area 6
barlow@pcuk.org
DC Liz Lovell
Sec Claire Lambie-Fryer

Beaufort Hunt (1932)
Area 9
beaufort@pcuk.org
DC Jane Humphreys
Sec Abigail Sharp

Bedale & West of Yore Hunt (1933)
Area 3
bedalewestofyores@pcuk.org
DC Alison Bartle
DC Karen Black
Sec Karen Black

Bedfordshire South (1935)
Area 12
bedfordshiresouth@pcuk.org
DC Sylvia Millard
Sec Jo Smith

Belvoir Hunt (1930)
Area 6
belvoir@pcuk.org
DC Tessa Buckley
Sec Debbie Weavers

Bennachie (1981)
Area 1
bennachie@pcuk.org
DC Fiona McLaren (acting)
Sec Jenna Dobbie

Berkeley Hunt (1930)
Area 9
berkeley@pcuk.org
DC Holly Dowsing
Sec Annabel Merrett

Berkeley Hunt South (1979)
Area 9
berkeleysouth@pcuk.org
DC Penny Stocks
DC Kim Wood
Sec Judy Hicks

Berwickshire Hunt (1932)
Area 19
berwickshire@pcuk.org
DC Jeanna Swan
Sec Fionna Henderson

Berwyn & Dee (1974)
Area 5
berwyndee@pcuk.org
DC Richard Hughes
Sec Bethan Roberts

Bicester & Warden Hill Hunt (1930)
Area 12
bicesterandwardenhill@pcuk.org
DC Julie Gordon
Sec Liz Willmott

Bisley and Sandown Chase (2013)
Area 13
bisley@pcuk.org
DC Sue Seers
Sec Anne-Marie Bibby

Blackburn & District (1965)
Area 4
blackburn@pcuk.org
DC Elaine Barker
Sec Helen Atkinson

Blackmore & Sparkford Vale Hunt (1930)
Area 14
blackmoreandsparkfordvale@pcuk.org
DC Veryan Gould
Sec Teona Hammond

Blankney Hunt (1938)
Area 6
blankney@pcuk.org
DC Anthea Jepson
Sec Kate Marshall

Braes of Derwent South (1982)
Area 2
braesofd@pcuk.org
DC Alex Emmerson
Sec Donna Cowie

Bramham Moor Hunt (1932)
Area 3
bramhammoor@pcuk.org
DC Elizabeth Hughes
Sec Amanda O'Reilly Weston

Brecon & Talybont Hunt (1950)
Area 10
breconandtalybont@pcuk.org
DC Ceri Bevan
DC Antonia Sheppard
Sec Amber Delahooke

Brocklesby Hunt (1944)
Area 6
brocklesby@pcuk.org
DC Janet Bowen
Sec Joanne Brown

Burghley (1958)
Area 6
burghley@pcuk.org
DC Laura Leicester
Sec Georgina Wilson

Burton Cheshire Forest Hunt (1948)
Area 5
burtoncheshireforest@pcuk.org
Sec Nicky Fryer

Burton Hunt (1947)
Area 6
burton@pcuk.org
DC Charlotte Fursdon
DC Rosie Newsam
Sec Emma Hore

Caithness (1973)
Area 1
caithness@pcuk.org
DC Debbie Pottinger
Sec Lisa Kennedy

Cambridgeshire Hunt (1934)
Area 8
cambridgeshire@pcuk.org
DC Emily Casey
Sec Wendy Ashcroft

Carmarthen Bay (1983)
Area 18
carmarthenbay@pcuk.org
DC Tim Joynson
Sec Vicky Joynson

Cattistock Hunt (1931)
Area 14
cattistock@pcuk.org
DC Tessa Mackenzie-Green
Sec Susan Harris

Cheshire Hunt North (1930)
Area 5
cheshirenorth@pcuk.org
DC Natalie Cliffe
Sec Julie Pedley

Cheshire Hunt South (1950)
Area 5
cheshiresouth@pcuk.org
DC Chris Kirby
Sec Karen Kirk

Chiddingfold (1930)
Area 13
chiddingfold@pcuk.org
DC Henrietta Paterson
Sec Lucy Jackson

Chiddingfold Farmers (1949)
Area 13
chiddingfoldfarmers@pcuk.org
DC Sarah Halsey
DC Clare Murdoch
Sec Sally Hayley

Chipping (1977)
Area 4
chipping@pcuk.org
DC Joanne Conlon
Sec Daphne Garment

Cleveland Hunt (1935)
Area 2
cleveland@pcuk.org
DC Vikki Clark
Sec Fiona Campbell

Cobham and Wimbledon (1951)
Area 11
wimbledon@pcuk.org
DC Cathy McGettigan
DC Elizabeth Jackson
Sec Michelle Agate

Cotley Hunt (1946)
Area 15
cotley@pcuk.org
DC Caroline Ford
DC Katrina Felgate
Sec Liz Russo

Cotswold Hunt (1930)
Area 9
cotswold@pcuk.org
DC Lucy Garbutt
Sec Debbie Wilkinson

Cotswold Vale Farmers' Hunt (1952)
Area 9
cotswoldvalefarmers@pcuk.org
DC Daniel Bingham
Sec Daniel Bingham

Cottesmore Hunt (1929)
Area 6
cottesmore@pcuk.org
DC Barbara Coulson
Sec Mary Tait

Cowdray Hunt (1936)
Area 13
cowdray@pcuk.org
DC Fiona Moss
Sec Tanya Carter

Craven Hunt (1929)
Area 14
craven@pcuk.org
DC Sophie Pope
Sec Liz Morris

Crawley & Horsham Hunt (1932)
Area 11
crawleyhorsham@pcuk.org
DC Julia Martin
Sec Angela Ellis

Crawley & Horsham Hunt South (1969)
Area 13
crawleyhorshamsouth@pcuk.org
DC Elisa Franks
Sec Karen Hall

Crickhowell & District (1982)
Area 10
crickhowell@pcuk.org
DC Hannah Laurent
Sec Rebecca Faulkner

Croome Hunt (1931)
Area 9
croome@pcuk.org
DC Sarah Roberts
Sec Jane Ogle

Cumberland Farmers' Hunt (South) (1943)
Area 2
cumberlandfarmerssouth@pcuk.org
DC Sarah Harden
Sec Fiona Veitch

Cumberland Farmers Hunt North (1949)
Area 2
cumberlandfarmersnorth@pcuk.org
DC Alison Gribbon
Sec Fiona Wharton

Cumberland Foxhounds (1957)
Area 2
cumberlandfoxhounds@pcuk.org
DC Lisa Fell
Sec Lisa Fell

Curre Hunt (1958)
Area 10
curre@pcuk.org
DC Jackie Budd
Sec Vicky Cardale

Cury Hunt (1979)
Area 16
cury@pcuk.org
DC Marilyn Ruberry
Sec Lisa Williams

Dalkeith & District (1963)
Area 19
dalkeith@pcuk.org
DC Karen Wotherspoon
Sec Yvonne Langley

Dare Valley (1999)
Area 10
darevalley@pcuk.org
DC Michelle Lewis
Sec Nicola Morgan

Dartmoor Hunt (1935)
Area 16
dartmoor@pcuk.org
DC Jane Mumford
Sec Fiona Green

Deeside (1977)
Area 1
deeside@pcuk.org
DC Mary Robertson
Sec Patricia Graham

Derwent Hunt (1963)
Area 3
derwent@pcuk.org
DC Lynne Harrison
Sec Tammy Wright

Deveron (1973)
Area 1
deveron@pcuk.org
DC Alice Paterson
DC Val Raich
Sec Emma Miller

Devon & Somerset (1931)
Area 15
devonsomerset@pcuk.org
DC Sue Mccanlis
Sec Sarah Daniel

Dinas Powys (1975)
Area 10
dinaspowis@pcuk.org
DC Clare Roberts
Sec Ceri Rowlands

Dolgellau & District (2009)
Area 5
dolgellau@pcuk.org
DC Sarah Williams
Sec Melanie Brookes-Jones

Duke of Buccleuch's Hunt (1931)
Area 19
dukeofbuccleuchs@pcuk.org
DC Emma McCallum
Sec Karen Marshall

Dulverton West Foxhounds (North Molton) Hunt (1957)
Area 15
dulvertonwestfoxhoundsnorthmolton@pcuk.org
DC Sara Gallagher
Sec Donna Wright

Dumfriesshire Hunt (1932)
Area 19
dumfriesshire@pcuk.org
DC Nicola Kerr
Sec Samantha Mungall

Dwyfor (2001)
Area 5
dwyfor@pcuk.org
DC Francess Ifan
Sec Hope Filby

East Aberdeenshire (Buchan) (1977)
Area 1
eastaberdeenshirebuchan@pcuk.org
DC Lesley Anderson
Sec Donna Wiseman

East Antrim (1965)
Area 17
eastantrim@pcuk.org
DC Hayley Cunningham
Sec Kathy Morrow

East Cheshire (1960)
Area 5
eastcheshire@pcuk.org
DC Geoff Bell
Sec Heather Pearson

East Cleveland (1975)
Area 2
eastcleveland@pcuk.org
DC Andrea Green
Sec Beverley Clarkson

East Cornwall Hunt (1931)
Area 16
eastcornwall@pcuk.org
DC Helen Moore
Sec Claire Mollet

East Devon Hunt (1932)
Area 15
eastdevon@pcuk.org
DC Thomasina Wilmington
Sec Sarah Miller

East Down (1936)
Area 17
eastdown@pcuk.org
DC Fran Rowlatt-McCormick
DC Catherine Sharvin
Sec Christine Crozier

East Essex Hunt (1932)
Area 8
eastessex@pcuk.org
DC Kate Tabor
Sec Clair Dawson

East Hertfordshire Hunt (1931)
Area 12
easthertfordshire@pcuk.org
DC Trish Griffiths
Sec Lisa Garrad

East Kent Hunt (1933)
Area 11
eastkent@pcuk.org
DC Michelle Dingle
Sec Katie Latchford

East Lothian (1952)
Area 19
eastlothian@pcuk.org
DC Sara O'Connor
Sec Lois Bayne-Jardine

East Stirlingshire (1970)
Area 1
eaststirlingshire@pcuk.org
DC Judi Dunn
DC Kaeli Pettigrew
Sec Kaeli Pettigrew

East Sussex (1931)
Area 11
eastsussex@pcuk.org
DC Clare Bassett
Sec Amanda Norman

Easton Harriers Hunt (1935)
Area 8
easton@pcuk.org
DC Helena Packshaw
Sec Tracy Sayer

Edinburgh (1994)
Area 19
edinburgh@pcuk.org
DC Sarah McLean
DC Katie Pier
Sec Kellyanne Miller

Eggesford Hunt (1951)
Area 16
eggesford@pcuk.org
DC Deborah Handley
Sec Sue Turner

Eglinton Hunt (1933)
Area 19
eglinton@pcuk.org
DC Pamela Johnstone
Sec Saskia Yates

Enfield Chace Hunt (1933)
Area 8
enfieldchace@pcuk.org
DC Katrina Midgley
Sec Sally Hawes

Eridge Hunt (1935)
Area 11
eridge@pcuk.org
DC Sarah Porter
Sec Sarah Davies

Eskdale (1974)
Area 19
eskdale@pcuk.org
DC Alison Brown
Sec Sharon Young

Essex & Suffolk Hunt (1939)
Area 8
essexsuffolk@pcuk.org
DC Mary Thornley
Sec Sophie Bardrick

Essex Farmers (1960)
Area 8
essexfarmers@pcuk.org
DC Philippa Howie
Sec Jo Wood

Essex Hunt North (1956)
Area 8
essexnorth@pcuk.org
DC Oriel Gordon
DC Georgie Mackley
Sec Sarah Nelmes

Essex Union (1930)
Area 8
essexunion@pcuk.org
DC Emma Whiteford
Sec Shireen Clark

Essex Union South (1968)
Area 8
essexunionsouth@pcuk.org
DC Gerry Drummond
Sec Joanna Adams

Fermanagh Harriers (1956)
Area 17
fermanagh@pcuk.org
DC Frances Rolston Bruce
Sec Denise Owens

Fernie Hunt (1929)
Area 6
fernie@pcuk.org
DC Rachel Harrison
Sec Claire Robinson

Fife Hunt (1946)
Area 1
fife@pcuk.org
DC Sue Cheape
Sec Jane MacLeod

Fitzwilliam Hunt (1930)
Area 6
fitzwilliam@pcuk.org
DC Philippa Patel
Sec Sylvie Hall

Flamstead (1973)
Area 12
flamstead@pcuk.org
DC Rosie Grimston
Sec Gemma Issott

Flint & Denbigh Hunt (1947)
Area 5
flintdenbigh@pcuk.org
DC Bethan Jones
Sec Iona Pierce

Forth Valley (1960)
Area 1
forthvalley@pcuk.org
DC Hilary McKelvie
Sec Emma McAuley

Four Burrow Hunt (1935)
Area 16
fourburrow@pcuk.org
DC Karen Tozer
Sec Gill Whetman

Furness & District (1949)
Area 4
furness@pcuk.org
DC Cathy Almond
DC Rachel Cooper
Sec Lindsey Wiejak

Fylde & District (1957)
Area 4
fylde@pcuk.org
Sec Alanna Richardson

Galloway (1957)
Area 19
galloway@pcuk.org
DC Joss Drummond
Sec Louise Jamieson

Garth Hunt (1930)
Area 13
garth@pcuk.org
DC Anne-Marie Peries
Sec Heidi Maxwell

Garth South (1965)
Area 13
garthsouth@pcuk.org
DC Candy Burnyeat
Sec Becky Gibbons

Glaisdale Hunt (1966)
Area 3
glaisdale@pcuk.org
DC Jenny Fowles
Sec Gill Kidd

Glamorgan Hunt (1949)
Area 10
glamorgan@pcuk.org
DC Annie Whitehouse
Sec Julia Jarvis

Glenrothes (1978)
Area 1
glenrothes@pcuk.org
DC Alison Peden
Sec Fiona MacGregor

Glossop & District (1972)
Area 4
glossop@pcuk.org
DC Stacey Ogden
Sec Louise Ratcliffe

Goathland Hunt (1957)
Area 3
goathland@pcuk.org
DC Lisa Smith
Sec Samantha McCarthy

Gogerddan (1956)
Area 18
gogerddan@pcuk.org
DC Katie Bevan
Sec Sarah Jones

Golden Valley Hunt (1946)
Area 10
goldenvalley@pcuk.org
DC Tracey Garrett
DC Julie Archer
Sec Julie Archer

Goodwood (1989)
Area 13
goodwood@pcuk.org
DC Samantha Garry
Sec Gwen Parker

Grafton Hunt (1930)
Area 12
grafton@pcuk.org
DC Carolyn Harvey
Sec Joanna Lee

Grove Hunt (1945)
Area 6
grove@pcuk.org
DC Emma Marsden
Sec Katie Sanderson

Guernsey (1954)
Area 14
guernsey@pcuk.org
DC Jayne Lane
Sec Brenda De Carteret

Gwynedd (1966)
Area 5
gwynedd@pcuk.org
DC Ioan Doyle
Sec Nia Williams

Hambledon Hunt (North) (1946)
Area 13
hambledonnorth@pcuk.org
DC Sarah Mosse
Sec Marianne Fisher

Hampshire Hunt (1931)
Area 13
hh@pcuk.org
DC Nicola Rowsell
DC Lucy Hunter
Sec Lara Mann

Haydock Park (1958)
Area 4
haydockpark@pcuk.org
DC Michelle Beard
Sec Sharon Brereton

Heart of England (1975)
Area 7
heartofengland@pcuk.org
DC Shelley Mitchell
Sec Sue Hall

Hertfordshire Hunt (1934)
Area 12
hertfordshire@pcuk.org
DC Debbie Fogden
Sec Orla Hinds

Heythrop Hunt (1931)
Area 9
heythrop@pcuk.org
DC Kate Campion
DC Nicola Browne
Sec Sarah Taylor

High Peak Hunt (1932)
Area 6
highpeak@pcuk.org
DC Ruth Taylor
Sec Molly Briddon

Holcombe Hunt (1931)
Area 4
holcombe@pcuk.org
DC Lesley Jenkinson
Sec Claire Lockett

Holderness Hunt (1946)
Area 3
holderness@pcuk.org
DC Pamela Ireland
Sec Deborah Bayliss

Hursley Hunt (1946)
Area 14
hursley@pcuk.org
DC Lucinda Hill
Sec Sheila Robertson

Hurworth Hunt (1933)
Area 3
hurworth@pcuk.org
DC Louisa Hunter
Sec Louisa Hunter

Inverness-shire (1964)
Area 1
inverness-shire@pcuk.org
DC Elizabeth Ashburn
Sec Carlann Mackay

Irfon & Tywi (2001)
Area 10
irfontywi@pcuk.org
DC Jo Price
Sec Jo Price

Isle of Man (1958)
Area 4
isleofman@pcuk.org
DC Alice Corrin
Sec Carolyn Lace

Isle of Mull (1976)
Area 19
isleofmull@pcuk.org
DC Flora Corbett
Sec Eilidh Munro

Isle of Sheppey (1984)
Area 11
isleofsheppey@pcuk.org
DC Sarah Shave
Sec Zoe Jenkins

Isle of Wight (1931)
Area 13
isleofwight@pcuk.org
DC Samantha Martin
Sec Nancy Hawkins

Iveagh (1962)
Area 17
iveagh@pcuk.org
DC Vanne Campbell
Sec Cathy Robinson

Ivel Valley (1981)
Area 12
ivelvalley@pcuk.org
DC Caroline Warwick
DC Jessica Kelly
Sec Julie McMillan

Jersey Drag Hunt (1952)
Area 14
jerseydrag@pcuk.org
DC Pippa Webster
Sec Sophie Oliveira

Kenfig Hill (2017)
Area 10
kenfighill@pcuk.org
DC Alison Davies
Sec Laura Terry

Kent Border (1980)
Area 11
kentborder@pcuk.org
DC Jo True
Sec Katherine Ingleby

Killultagh Old Rock & Chichester Harriers (1959)
Area 17
killultagh@pcuk.org
DC Noreen Fitzpatrick
Sec Jenny Rollins

Kincardineshire (1963)
Area 1
kincardineshire@pcuk.org
DC Janice Carnegie
Sec Gill Carnegie

Lamerton Hunt (1954)
Area 16
lamerton@pcuk.org
DC Sue Ryan
Sec Sally Watton

Lanark & Upperward (1974)
Area 19
lanarkupperward@pcuk.org
DC Margaret Young
Sec Kirstie MacGillivray

Lanarkshire & Renfrewshire Hunt (1934)
Area 19
lanarkshirerenfrewshire@pcuk.org
DC Tom Alexander

Lancaster & District (1964)
Area 4
lancaster@pcuk.org
DC Emma Walsh
Sec Victoria Matichecchia

Lauderdale Hunt (1982)
Area 19
lauderdale@pcuk.org
DC Alex Mundell
Sec Gillian And Ian Mcfadyen

Ledbury Hunt (1932)
Area 9
ledbury@pcuk.org
DC Lucy Middlecote
DC Sophie Jones
Sec Katie Baker

Linlithgow & Stirlingshire (1931)
Area 19
linlithgowstirlingshire@pcuk.org
DC Clare McLay
DC Claire Leitch
Sec Caroline Courtney

Littleport & District (1970)
Area 8
littleport@pcuk.org
DC Chris Hughes
Sec Katherine Hughes

Llandeilo & District (1982)
Area 18
llandeilo@pcuk.org
DC Janet Daniels
Sec Karen Goss

Llangeinor Hunt (1960)
Area 10
llangeinor@pcuk.org
DC Rachel Pugh
DC Lesley Kemeys
Sec Louise Owen

Llangibby Hunt (1954)
Area 10
llangibby@pcuk.org
DC Sara Owen
DC Caron Bennett
Sec Karla Brake

Lord Leconfield Hunt (1934)
Area 13
lordleconfield@pcuk.org
DC Clare Emery
DC Sue Coombe Tennant
Sec Carrie Schroter

Ludlow Hunt (1929)
Area 7
ludlow@pcuk.org
DC Louise Powell
Sec Jean Yarnold

Malvern (1940)
Area 9
malvern@pcuk.org
DC Maria Hardy
Sec Amanda Allsop

Mendip Farmers' Hunt (1930)
Area 14
mendipfarmers@pcuk.org
DC Clea Frost
DC Ruth Dadswell
Sec Diana Tincknell

Meynell Hunt (1929)
Area 6
meynell@pcuk.org
DC Fiona Roobottom
Sec Lesley Cutler

Mid Antrim (1971)
Area 17
midantrim@pcuk.org
DC Trudy Woolsey
Sec Elizabeth Graham

Mid Devon Hunt (1937)
Area 16
middevon@pcuk.org
DC Harriet Every
Sec Roo Haywood Smith

Mid Surrey (1931)
Area 11
midsurrey@pcuk.org
DC Gina Kitchener
Sec Wendy Wrist

Middleton Hunt (1932)
Area 3
middleton@pcuk.org
Sec Sarah Barker

Middleton Hunt (East Side) (1975)
Area 3
middletoneastside@pcuk.org
DC Helen Milner
Sec Kim Brompton

Minchinhampton (1969)
Area 9
minchinhampton@pcuk.org
DC Julie Crew
Sec Thandi Rudin

Monmouthshire (1931)
Area 10
monmouthshire@pcuk.org
DC Susan Fairweather
Sec Jessica Tod

Moray & Nairn (1948)
Area 1
moraynairn@pcuk.org
DC Hayley Ingram
Sec Joanne McRae

Morpeth Hunt (1937)
Area 2
morpeth@pcuk.org
DC Michelle Macaulay
Sec Gail Jeffrey

Neath (1968)
Area 18
neath@pcuk.org
DC Ceinwen Howells
Sec Rhiannon Phillips

New Forest Hunts (1932)
Area 14
newforest@pcuk.org
DC Gill Sporne
Sec Susan Hogarth

Newcastle & North Durham (1961)
Area 2
newcastlenorthdurham@pcuk.org
DC Sheila Clifford
Sec Melanie Boatman

Newmarket & Thurlow Hunt (1940)
Area 8
newmarketthurlow@pcuk.org
DC Tessa Vestey
DC Ginny Faire
Sec Jilly Beaton

Nithsdale (1978)
Area 19
nithsdale@pcuk.org
DC Philippa Barnes
Sec Philippa Barnes

North Argyll (1968)
Area 1
northargyll@pcuk.org
DC Eilidh Betts
DC Janice Burnip
Sec Grace Neilson

North Cornwall (1932)
Area 16
northcornwall@pcuk.org
DC Anita Foulsham
Sec Louise Dally

North Cotswold Hunt (1930)
Area 9
northcotswold@pcuk.org
DC Jackie Ferguson
DC Paula Leavy
Sec Paula Leavy

North Derry (1950)
Area 17
northderry@pcuk.org
DC Debra Beacham
DC Pauline Lusby
Sec Nikki Killen

North Down (1939)
Area 17
northdown@pcuk.org
DC Evelyn Dunlop
Sec Sandra Vollands

North Herefordshire Hunt (1951)
Area 9
northherefordshire@pcuk.org
DC Caroline Queen
DC Rachel Barrett
Sec Joanna White

North Norfolk (1935)
Area 8
northnorfolk@pcuk.org
DC Ben Westgate
Sec Pauline Tann

North Northumberland Hunt (1955)
Area 2
northnorthumberland@pcuk.org
DC Julia Frost
Sec Jane Mason

North Shropshire Hunt (1929)
Area 7
northshropshire@pcuk.org
DC Ann Gregory

North Staffordshire Hunt (1931)
Area 7
northstaffordshire@pcuk.org
DC Natalie Massey
Sec Gillian Fox

North Warwickshire (1931)
Area 7
northwarwickshire@pcuk.org
DC Elizabeth Grindal
Sec Linda Wolverson

North West Kent (1947)
Area 11
northwestkent@pcuk.org
DC Fiona Scott
Sec Jane Collins

Oakley Hunt North (1981)
Area 12
oakleynorth@pcuk.org
DC Christine Cinnamond
Sec Clare Goduti

Oakley Hunt West (1931)
Area 12
oakleywest@pcuk.org
DC Wendy Barnes
Sec Fiona Falle

Old Berkeley Hunt (Chilterns) (1968)
Area 12
oldberkeleychilterns@pcuk.org
DC Emma Stratford
Sec Kate Blankertz

Old Berkeley Hunt (Hughenden) (1968)
Area 12
oldberkeleyhughenden@pcuk.org
DC Amanda Bacon
Sec Sam Moody

Old Berkeley Hunt (North) (1959)
Area 12
oldberkeleynorth@pcuk.org
DC Sue Palmer-Shaw
DC Catherine Shine
Sec Sarah Molony

Old Berkeley Hunt (South) (1959)
Area 12
oldberkeleysouth@pcuk.org
DC Kim Williams
Sec Justine Brett-Chinnery

Old Berkshire Hunt (1943)
Area 9
oldberkshire@pcuk.org
DC Alison Hargreaves
DC Joanna Lambert
Sec Joy Wilson

Old Surrey & Burstow Hunt (1929)
Area 11
oldsurreyburstow@pcuk.org
DC Caroline Matthews
Sec Amanda Bernard

Orkney (1963)
Area 1
orkney@pcuk.org
DC Carole Linklater
Sec Susan Bain

Oxenholme (1936)
Area 4
oxenholme@pcuk.org
DC Jillian Clark
Sec Karen Barnes

Parc Howard (1993)
Area 18
parchoward@pcuk.org
DC Catherine Roberts

Peak (1959)
Area 4
peak@pcuk.org
DC Danielle Dawson
Sec Sarah Booth

Peebles Tweeddale (1975)
Area 19
peeblestweeddale@pcuk.org
DC Kate Philipps
DC Maggie Carson
Sec Nicola Spurway

Pembrokeshire Hunt (1935)
Area 18
pembrokeshire@pcuk.org
DC Janet Luke
DC Jill Ridge
Sec Sally Evans

Pendle Forest & Craven Hunt (1935)
Area 4
pendleforestcraven@pcuk.org
DC Elizabeth Bower
Sec Katy Edwards

Pentyrch (1953)
Area 10
pentyrch@pcuk.org
DC Lynda Evans
Sec Sue DuCroq

Percy Hunt (1947)
Area 2
percy@pcuk.org
DC Sue Haughie
Sec Esther Haughie

Perth Hunt (1946)
Area 1
perth@pcuk.org
DC Ashley Sinclair
Sec Jayne Lamont

Petersfield (1977)
Area 13
petersfield@pcuk.org
DC Gill Ibbott
DC Jane Fletcher
Sec Julie Gordon

Polden Hills (1975)
Area 15
poldenhills@pcuk.org
DC Kim Tripp
Sec Lorraine Wells

Poole & District (1973)
Area 14
poole@pcuk.org
DC Sarah Chandler
DC Cheryl Dennett
Sec Lynne Seare

Portman Hunt (1931)
Area 14
portman@pcuk.org
DC Linda Jones
DC Catherine Langham
Sec Kirstie Thompson

Puckeridge Hunt (1931)
Area 8
puckeridge@pcuk.org
DC Sophie Payne
Sec Jennifer Snell

Puckeridge Hunt Western (1946)
Area 8
puckeridgewestern@pcuk.org
DC Rachel Welbourne
Sec Sandra Laithwaite

Pytchley Hunt (1930)
Area 7
pytchley@pcuk.org
DC Sarah Jane Page
Sec Elise Paybody

Quantock Hunt (1933)
Area 15
quantock@pcuk.org
DC Frances Barker
DC Kathryn Sims
Sec Kaye Hill

Quorn Hunt (1929)
Area 6
quorn@pcuk.org
DC Sue Henton
Sec Carol Davis

Radnor & West Hereford Hunt (1935)
Area 10
radnor@pcuk.org
DC Penny Corbett
Sec Beverley Waygood

Rockwood Harriers (1930)
Area 3
rockwood@pcuk.org
DC Ann Shepherd
Sec Ann Shepherd

Romney Marsh (1948)
Area 11
romneymarsh@pcuk.org
DC Christine Makin
Sec Sarah Hues

Ross-shire (1959)
Area 1
ross-shire@pcuk.org
DC Kelly Skinner
Sec Jane Wilson

Route Hunt (1958)
Area 17
route@pcuk.org
DC Anne-Marie Carr
DC Fred White
Sec Anne-Marie Carr

Royal Artillery (1946)
Area 14
ra@pcuk.org
DC Judy Hyson
Sec Jenny Read

Rufford Hunt (1948)
Area 6
rufford@pcuk.org
DC Debbie Dawson
Sec Diane Shepheard

Ryburn Valley (1970)
Area 3
ryburnvalley@pcuk.org
DC Liz Dunn
Sec Louise Jones

Saddleworth & District (1960)
Area 4
saddleworth@pcuk.org
DC Alison Prenty
Sec Gillian Morrell

Scunthorpe & District (1968)
Area 6
scunthorpe@pcuk.org
DC Helen Ritchie
Sec James Rowland

Seavington (1974)
Area 15
seavington@pcuk.org
DC Paul And Pip Bailey
Sec Lucy Atherton

Sennybridge & District (1974)
Area 10
sennybridge@pcuk.org
DC Georgina Philipson-Stow
Sec Susan Moore

Seskinore Harriers (1974)
Area 17
seskinore@pcuk.org
DC Jenna Coote
DC Mandy McQuade
Sec Bernie Murnaghan

Silverton Hunt (1931)
Area 15
silverton@pcuk.org
DC Claire Cook

Sinnington Hunt (1946)
Area 3
sinnington@pcuk.org
DC Rosemary Cordingley
Sec Emma Du Boulay

Sir W W Wynn's Hunt (1929)
Area 5
sirwwwynns@pcuk.org
DC Belinda Hutchinson Smith
DC Joanna Adams
Sec Jane Courtney

Soham & District (1976)
Area 8
soham@pcuk.org
DC Sally Green
Sec Katie Mercer

South & West Wilts Hunt (1934)
Area 14
southwestwilts@pcuk.org
DC Henrietta Woodward
Sec Sarah Cutler

South Berkshire (1930)
Area 13
southberkshire@pcuk.org
DC Hayley Dunstan
Sec Emily Mumby

South Devon Hunt (Moorland) (1973)
Area 16
southdevonmoorland@pcuk.org
DC Fiona Froy
Sec Kate Reece

South Devon West (1932)
Area 16
southdevonwest@pcuk.org
DC Heather Venmore
Sec Pauline Bridge

South Dorset Hunt (1931)
Area 14
southdorset@pcuk.org
DC Claire Ferguson
Sec Alice Haw

South Durham Hunt (1947)
Area 2
southdurham@pcuk.org
DC Friedl Hutchinson
Sec Emma-Kate Darnton

South Hereford and Ross Harriers (1944)
Area 9
southherefordross@pcuk.org
DC Kirstie Macfarlane
Sec Kirstie Macfarlane

South Hertfordshire (1963)
Area 12
southhertfordshire@pcuk.org
DC Samantha Branley
Sec Melanie Reid

South Norfolk (1935)
Area 8
southnorfolk@pcuk.org
DC Aidan Taylor
DC Lizzie Meadows
Sec Aline Turner

South Northumberland (1931)
Area 2
southnorthumberland@pcuk.org
DC Heather McDonald
Sec Helen Proctor

South Nottinghamshire (1939)
Area 6
southnottinghamshire@pcuk.org
DC Jane Clayton
Sec Janet Rycroft

South Oxfordshire Hunt (South) (1930)
Area 12
southoxfordshiresouth@pcuk.org
DC Louise Pope
Sec Verity Matthews

South Oxfordshire Hunt Central (1961)
Area 12
southoxfordshirecentral@pcuk.org
DC Tamsin Woods
Sec Lucy Minford

South Pembrokeshire & Cresselly Hunt (1958)
Area 18
southpembrokeshire@pcuk.org
DC Jacqui Morgan
Sec Caroline Elsdon

South Pool (1963)
Area 16
southpool@pcuk.org
DC Victoria Goodlad
Sec Janet Widdicombe

South Shropshire Hunt (1929)
Area 7
southshropshire@pcuk.org
DC Tor Smith
Sec Verity Criddle

South Staffordshire Hunt (1931)
Area 7
southstaffordshire@pcuk.org
DC Barbara Smith
Sec Katharine Egerton

South Trent (1963)
Area 6
southtrent@pcuk.org
DC Jane Foster
Sec Genevieve Stewart-Smith

South Wold Hunt North (1950)
Area 6
southwoldnorth@pcuk.org
DC Krystina Alex
DC Lindy Robertson
Sec Karen Elliott

Southdown Hunt (East) (1976)
Area 11
southdowneast@pcuk.org
DC (Caroline) Anne Cook
Sec Candy Robbins

Southdown Hunt West (1936)
Area 11
southdownwest@pcuk.org
DC Tracy Vardy
Sec Caroline Duval

Spooners & West Dartmoor (1967)
Area 16
spooners@pcuk.org
DC Rebecca Townsend
Sec Julia McDermott

St Davids & District (1984)
Area 18
saintdavids@pcuk.org
DC Rob Harper
Sec Judith Harper

Staff College & Sandhurst (1953)
Area 13
staffcollege@pcuk.org
DC Gillian Chambers
DC Jane Austen Armstrong
Sec Cate Hooper

Staintondale Hunt (1958)
Area 3
staintondale@pcuk.org
DC Marie Mc Faul
Sec Victoria Verrill

Stevenstone & Torrington Farmers Hunt (1945)
Area 16
stevenstone@pcuk.org
DC Michelle Harding
Sec Sarah Ellis

Stewartry (1965)
Area 19
stewartry@pcuk.org
DC Sarah Burton
Sec Julia Graham

Strathblane & District (1949)
Area 19
strathblane@pcuk.org
DC Madeleine Franzmann
DC Emily Hedgecoe
Sec Isabelle Thomson

Strathearn (1949)
Area 1
strathearn@pcuk.org
DC Jane Cepok
Sec Elaine Johnson

Stroud (1978)
Area 9
stroud@pcuk.org
DC Catie Howard
Sec Vicki Birtwhistle

Suffolk Hunt (1932)
Area 8
suffolk@pcuk.org
DC Jane Crawford
Sec Adele Cutler

Surrey Union (1935)
Area 11
surreyunion@pcuk.org
DC Deborah Winchester
Sec Tania Forsdick

Swansea & District (1949)
Area 18
swansea@pcuk.org
DC Ann Walter
Sec Jennifer Gregory

Syston (1964)
Area 14
syston@pcuk.org
DC Marie Kelly
Sec Claire Rudge

Tanatside Hunt (1935)
Area 5
tanatside@pcuk.org
DC Leanne Garvey
DC Susie Wilkinson
Sec Saskia Jones-Perrott

Taunton Vale (1932)
Area 15
tauntonvale@pcuk.org
DC Elizabeth Crew
Sec Rachel Holden

Taunton Vale Harriers (1972)
Area 15
tauntonvaleharriers@pcuk.org
DC Jacquie Rowcliffe
Sec Angela Heard

Tedworth Hunt (1930)
Area 14
tedworth@pcuk.org
DC Joss Dalrymple
DC Sophie Dalrymple
Sec Lorraine Perry

Teme Valley Hunt (1962)
Area 10
temevalley@pcuk.org
DC Gwynneth Lloyd
Sec Mandy Baldwin

Tetcott & South Tetcott Hunts (1953)
Area 16
tetcottsouthtetcotts@pcuk.org
DC Diana Stevens
Sec Penny Gingell

Thetford Chase (1961)
Area 8
thetfordchase@pcuk.org
DC Laura Clear
Sec Zoe Southgate

Tickham Hunt (1937)
Area 11
tickham@pcuk.org
DC Michelle Graham
Sec Jo Mitchelhill

Tiverton Hunt (1946)
Area 15
tiverton@pcuk.org
DC Natalie Wedden
Sec Julie Heal

Tivyside (1960)
Area 18
tivyside@pcuk.org
DC Helen Williams
Sec Louise Parry

Tredegar Farmers Hunt (1948)
Area 10
tredegarfarmers@pcuk.org
DC Marie Christopher
Sec Sue Bacon

Tullylagan (1976)
Area 17
tullylagan@pcuk.org
DC Colleen Glasgow
DC Christine Kennedy
Sec Jillian O'Neill

Tynedale Hunt (1971)
Area 2
tynedale@pcuk.org
DC Wendy Murray
Sec Lesley Walby

United Pack (1932)
Area 7
unitedpack@pcuk.org
DC Sally Williams
Sec Nicola Fitter

Vale of Aylesbury Hunt (1931)
Area 12
valeofaylesbury@pcuk.org
DC Rachel Good
Sec Kate Rolfe

Vale of Clettwr (1975)
Area 18
valeofclettwr@pcuk.org
DC Michael Coleman
Sec Alyson Adair

Vale of Taf (1978)
Area 18
valeoftaf@pcuk.org
DC Jacqui Kedward
Sec Jacqui Kedward

Vale of York (1976)
Area 3
valeofyork@pcuk.org
DC Christine Dalby
Sec Barbara Lister

Vine (1934)
Area 13
vine@pcuk.org
DC Madeline Lawson
Sec Sarah Birkett

VWH Hunt (1930)
Area 9
vwh@pcuk.org
DC Georgie Davies
Sec Jo Ramage

Waen-y-Llyn (1974)
Area 5
waen-y-llyn@pcuk.org
DC Dani Tanton
Sec Helen Lakin

Walpole & District (2006)
Area 8
walpole@pcuk.org
DC Jacky Jillings
Sec Jacky Jillings

Warwickshire Hunt (1932)
Area 7
warwickshire@pcuk.org
DC Susan Dancer
Sec Pauline Collings

Waveney Harriers (1934)
Area 8
waveney@pcuk.org
DC Judy Haythornthwaite

West Cumberland (1959)
Area 2
westcumberland@pcuk.org
DC Sarah Irving
DC Christen Hilton
Sec Karin Wood

West Hants (1967)
Area 14
westhants@pcuk.org
DC Susan Whitlock
Sec Emma Pink

West Kent (Sevenoaks) (1930)
Area 11
westkentsevenoaks@pcuk.org
DC Anne MIlls
Sec Helen Giddings

West Kent Meopham (1972)
Area 11
westkentmeopham@pcuk.org
DC Julie Dinnis
Sec Lizzie Carter-Griffiths

West Lancashire County (1933)
Area 4
westlancashirecounty@pcuk.org
DC Fiona Lace
Sec Elaine Wall

West Lancashire Ince Blundell (1933)
Area 4
westlancashireinceblundell@pcuk.org
DC Michelle Dudley
Sec Fiona Clague

West Midlands (1975)
Area 7
westmidlands@pcuk.org
DC Mandy Keenan
Sec Amy Farley

West Norfolk Hunt (1935)
Area 8
westnorfolk@pcuk.org
DC Juliet Case
Sec Sophie Edwards

West Perthshire (1974)
Area 1
westperthshire@pcuk.org
DC David Lindsay

West Somerset (1956)
Area 15
westsomerset@pcuk.org
DC Karin Harwood
Sec Kali Martin

West Warwickshire (1961)
Area 7
westwarwickshire@pcuk.org
DC Caroline Chadwick
Sec Lucy Jackson

Western Hunt (1935)
Area 16
western@pcuk.org
DC Diana Hardy
Sec Sarah Tieken

Western Isles (1981)
Area 1
westernIsles@pcuk.org
DC Mairi Fellows
Sec Ann Smith

Weston Harriers Hunt (1932)
Area 15
weston@pcuk.org
DC Lyn Bugler
Sec Karen Pinn

Whaddon Chase (1931)
Area 12
whaddonchase@pcuk.org
DC Nicola Thorne
Sec Christine Hickey

Wheatland Hunt (1946)
Area 7
wheatland@pcuk.org
DC Dawn Moreton
Sec Caroline Williamson

Wheelton & District (1974)
Area 4
wheelton@pcuk.org
DC Ian Nolan-Plunkett
Sec Kate Cartwright

Wilton Hunt (1933)
Area 14
wilton@pcuk.org
DC Sally Lefroy
Sec Fran Lockyer

Wokingham (1974)
Area 13
wokingham@pcuk.org
DC Julie Browne
Sec Suzy Turner

Woodland Hunt (1950)
Area 12
woodland@pcuk.org
DC Emma Dag
Sec Juliet Barnett

Woodland Pytchley Hunt (1931)
Area 6
woodlandpytchley@pcuk.org
DC Lucie Burges-Lumdsen
Sec Tara Baker

Worcestershire Hunt (1931)
Area 9
worcestershire@pcuk.org
DC Eve Wood
DC Jayne Whitbread
Sec Rebecca Briggs

Wormwood Scrubs (1992)
Area 12
wormwoodscrubs@pcuk.org

Wylye Valley (1952)
Area 14
wylyevalley@pcuk.org
DC Miles Toulson-Clarke

Wyndham (1964)
Area 2
wyndham@pcuk.org
DC Maureen White
Sec Carole Smith

Wyre Forest (1975)
Area 9
wyreforest@pcuk.org
DC Alison Vincent
Sec Catherine MacDonald

Ynysybwl (1976)
Area 10
ynysybwl@pcuk.org
DC Beverley Haddock
Sec Emma Davies

York & Ainsty North (1950)
Area 3
yorkainstynorth@pcuk.org
DC Barbara Birchall
Sec Helen Vesty

York & Ainsty South (1959)
Area 3
yorkainstysouth@pcuk.org
DC Gill Chivers
Sec Suzanna Barker

Zetland Hunt (1932)
Area 2
zetland@pcuk.org
DC Andrea Bartlett
Sec Jeanette Crompton

PONY CLUB CENTRES IN THE UK

Abbotsholme Equestrian Centre (Area 7)
Simon Rusco-Price, Abbotsholme School, Osmaston, Rocester, Uttoxeter, ST14 5BS, United Kingdom
01889 590217
katie.hickman@abbotsholme.co.uk

Accrington Riding Centre (Area 4)
Denise Holding, Rothwell Mill Farm, Miller Fold, Accrington, BB5 0NY, United Kingdom
01254 393563
lesleypaddy@hotmail.com

Achalone Activities (Area 1)
Marion Bain, North Achalone, Halkirk, KW12 6XA, United Kingdom
01847 831326
m-bain@sky.com

Acre Cliffe Equestrian Centre (Area 3)
Fiona Everall, Bradford Road, Otley, LS21 3DN, United Kingdom
01943 873912
enquiries@acrecliffe.co.uk

Aldborough Hall Equestrian Centre (Area 8)
Mary Garrett, Alborough Road, North Ilford, IG2 7TE, United Kingdom
02085 901433
aldboroughhall@gmail.com

Almond Equestrian (Area 6)
Jayne Almond, Chestnut Farm, Moor Hill, East Norton, LE7 9XF, United Kingdom
07808 555262
jayney.88@hotmail.com

Alstone Court Riding Establishment (Area 14)
Sally March, Alstone Lane, Highbridge, TA9 3DS, United Kingdom
07702 392120
alstonecourt@live.co.uk

Angel Riding Centre (Area 3)
Debbie Murphy, Morton Lane, Hambleton, Selby, YO8 9LE, United Kingdom
07833 500333
Angellivery@live.co.uk

Annabelles Equestrian (Area 8)
Annabelle Block, Hall Farm, Church Road, Henstead, NR34 7LD, United Kingdom
01502 742303
annabelle_block@hotmail.com

Apollo Stables (Area 8)
Emma Spencer, Undley Road, Lakenheath, IP27 9BX, United Kingdom
01842 862000
apollostables1@gmail.com

Appletree Stud (Area 7)
Julie Scott, Claydon, Banbury, OX17 1ET, Unit Kingdom
07517 068354
pbscott31@sky.com

Argyll Adventure (Area 19)
Andrew Cameron, Argyll Adventure, Dalchenna Farm, Inveraray, PA32 8XT, Unite Kingdom
01499 302611
info@argylladventure.com

Ashdown Forest Riding Centre (Area 11)
Alison Crowe-Bell, King's Standing Farm, Bla Hill, Friars Gate, Crowborough, TN6 1XE, Unit Kingdom
07905 161967
ali.crowe31@yahoo.com

Asti Equestrian (Area 9)
Eve Rowland, Millaway Farm, Goosey, Faringdon, SN7 8PA, United Kingdom
01367 710288
astiequestrian@hotmail.com

Badshot Lea Equestrian Centre (Area 13)
John Hierons, Badshot Lea Equestrian Centre, Badshot Farm Lane, Badshot Lea, Farnham, GU9 9HY, United Kingdom
01252 312838
badshotleaec@gmail.com

Ballawhetstone (Area 4)
Stella Hampton, Ballawhetstone Farm, Douglas Road, IM9 4ED, United Kingdom
01624 825778
ballawhetstonestables@manx.net

Bank House Equestrian (Area 2)
Nancy Atkinson, Little Salkeld, Penrith, CA10 1NN, United Kingdom
01768 881257
bankhouseequ@aol.com

Barguse Riding Centre (Area 16)
Lisa Todd, The Grange, Lockengate, St Austell, PL26 8RU, United Kingdom
01208 831817
info@barguse.co.uk

Barnfield Riding School (Area 13)
Patsy Ann Rose, Parkfields Road, Kingston upon Thames, KT2 5LL, United Kingdom
0208 546 3616
info@barnfieldridingschool.org

Barnfields Riding School (Area 8)
Daniel Burke, Sewardstone Road, Chingford, E4 7RH, United Kingdom
02085 295200
Barnfieldsridingstables@gmail.com

Barton Field Farm Equestrian Centre (Area 11)
Natalie Brown, Wingham Road, Littlebourne, Canterbury, CT3 1UP, United Kingdom
01227 722843
info@bffec.co.uk

Batley Hall Farm Riding Centre (Area 3)
Debbie Gaskin, Old Hall Road, Upper Batley, WF17 0AX, United Kingdom
01924 445067
equusridingclub@ymail.com

Baylands Equestrian Centre (Area 12)
Rebecca Whittingham, Stockwood Park, Luton, LU1 4BH, United Kingdom
01582 720766
email@baylands-equestrian.co.uk

Beaumont Grange Farm (Area 4)
Carol Hill, Black Castle Lane, Off Bottom Dale Road, Slyne with Hest, Nr Lancaster, LA2 6BG, United Kingdom
07904 208669
carolhillbeaumontgrange@gmail.com

Beaver Hall (Area 7)
Anne Pearn, Bradnop, Leek, ST13 7EZ, United Kingdom
01538 304433
horses@beaverhall.co.uk

Berkshire Riding Centre (Area 13)
Tim Lord, Crouch Lane, Winkfield, SL4 4TN, United Kingdom
01344 884992
tim@brc.uk.com

Bewerley Riding Centre (Area 3)
Silvia Schuler, The Cottage, Bewerley Old Hall, Pateley Bridge, Harrogate, HG3 5JA, United Kingdom
01423 712249
silvia@bewerleyriding.com

Bigland Hall Equine Group (Area 4)
Zara Myers, Brow Edge, Haverthwaite, Ulverston, LA12 8PB, United Kingdom
01539 530333
bookings@biglandhall.com

Birr House Riding Centre (Area 17)
Caroline McVeigh,81 Whinnery Hill, Craigantlet, Dundonald, BT16 1UA, United Kingdom
02890 425858
carolinemcveigh@btinternet.com

Bishton Hall Riding School (Area 7)
Sarah Brown, St. Bedes Preparatory School, Bishton Hall, Wolseley Bridge, Stafford, ST17 0XN, United Kingdom
01753 023053
bishtonponies@hotmail.co.uk

Blackdyke Farm Riding and Competition Centre (Area 2)
John Collier, Blackford, Carlisle, CA6 4EY, United Kingdom
01228 674633
john.collier@blackdykefarm.info

Blisworth Pony Club Centre (Area 12)
Kate Lee, New Tunnel Hill Farm, Stoke Road, Blisworth, NN7 3DB, United Kingdom
01604 858 041
katemadhouse@aol.com

Bold Heath Equestrian Centre (Area 4)
Janet and Mark Baker, Heath House Farm, Bold Heath, Widnes, WA8 3XT, United Kingdom
01514 245151
janet_e_baker@btconnect.com

Bourne Vale Riding Stables (Area 7)
Anna Cooper, Little Hardwick Road, Aldridge, Walsall, WS9 0SQ, United Kingdom
0121 353 7174
sales@bournevalestables.co.uk

Bourton Vale Equestrian Centre (Area 9)
Leanne Launchbury, College Farm, Stow Road, Bourton-on-the-Water, GL54 2HN, United Kingdom
01451 821101
bourtonvale@gmail.com

Bowdens Riding School at Balham (Area 15)
Annabelle Boucher, Balham Hill Farm, Chiselborough, South Petherton, TA14 6TY, United Kingdom
07946 805696
info@bowdensridingschool.co.uk

Bowlers Riding School (Area 4)
Mary Bowler,35 Brewery Lane, Freshfield, L37 7DY, United Kingdom
01704 872915
bowlersridingschool@hotmail.com

Bowlings Riding School (Area 18)
Janet Gibson, Rudbaxton, Haverfordwest, SA62 4DB, United Kingdom
01437 741407
bechaggar@aol.com

Brackenside Stables (Area 6)
Jayne Armstrong, Kirkby Lane, Woodhall Spa LN10 6YY, United Kingdom
01526 351398
brackenside@aol.com

Bradbourne Riding and Training Centre (Area 11)
Sarah Howe, Bradbourne Vale Road, Sevenoaks, TN13 3DH, United Kingdom
01732 453592
bradbourneponyclub@gmail.com

Braeside Equestrian Centre (Area 11)
Jane Driver, Nelson Park Road, St Margarets-at-Cliffe, Dover, CT15 6HL, United Kingdom
01304 852959
info@braeside.co.uk

Brampton Stables (Area 7)
Derick Ward, Stable Lane, Church Brampton, Northampton, NN6 8BH, United Kingdom
01604 842051
info@bramptonstables.com

Bridge End Equestrian (Area 3)
S-J Kendall, Bridge End Farm, Howe, Thirsk, YO7 4HT, United Kingdom
01845 565263 / 07866
sj@beequestrian.co.uk

Bridlewood Riding Centre (Area 5)
Sharon Houston, Maes-y-Coed Farm, Tyn-y-Morfa, Gwespyr, Nr Prestatyn, CH8 9JN, Unite Kingdom
01745 888922
mail@bridlewood.co.uk

Brimington Equestrian Centre (Area 6)
Tracey Johnston,130 Manor Road, Brimington, Chesterfield, S43 1NN, United Kingdom
01246 235465
brimingtonequestriancentre@yahoo.co.uk

Broadlands Riding Centre (Area 13)
Suzanne Stratford, Lower Paice Lane, Medstead, Alton, GU34 5PX, United Kingdom
01420 563382
suzanne@broadlandsgrouprda.org.uk

Brook Cottage Farm Riding School (Area 8)
Louise Seddon, Brook Cottage, Barley Croft End, Furneux Pelham, Buntingford, SG9 0LL, United Kingdom
07919 888655
louise.seddon@btinternet.com

Brook Stables (Area 12)
Jean Halls, Brook Stables, Fox Covert Farm, Fordfield Road, Millbrook, MK45 2HZ, United Kingdom
01525 840929
brookstables@btinternet.com

Brooksby Equestrian Centre (Area 6)
Donna Bates, Brooksby Melton College, Brooksby, Melton Mowbray, LE14 2LJ, United Kingdom
01664 855333
equestrian-centre@brooksbymelton.ac.uk

Broom Farm Riding (Area 1)
Aileen Donaldson, Broom Farm,, Stevenson,, KA20 3DD, United Kingdom
01294 465437
ladydog12.ad@googlemail.com

Broomhill Riding Centre (Area 1)
Christine Anderson - Dont Contact, Broomhill Farm, Fortrose, IV10 8SH, United Kingdom
01381 620214
broomhillridingcentre@gmail.com

Bryerley Springs Equestrian Centre (Area 12)
Kiki Salvers, Galley Lane, Great Brickhill, Milton Keynes, MK17 9AB, United Kingdom
01525 261823
admin@bryerleysprings.co.uk

Buckswood School Stables (Area 11)
Giles Sutton, Buckswood School, Rye Road, Guestling, TN35 4LT, United Kingdom
01424 813813
stables@buckswood.co.uk

Bulby Hall Equestrian Centre (Area 6)
Sue Bevan, Bulby Hall, Elsthorpe Road, Bulby, Bourne, PE10 0RU, United Kingdom
07483139232
susanfionabevan@outlook.com

Burley Villa School of Riding (Area 14)
Phil Cremer, Bashley Common Road, New Milton, BH25 5SH, United Kingdom
01425 610278
enquiry@burleyvilla.co.uk

Burnby Equestrian Centre (Area 3)
Susan Bargate, The Granary, Burnby EC, Burnby, YO42 1RS, United Kingdom
07850 664992
burnbyec@gmail.com

Burrows Lane Farm Riding School (Area 4)
Leanne Ryan, Burrows Lane, Eccleston, Prescot, L34 6JQ, United Kingdom
0151 430 0046
burrowslanefarm@live.co.uk

Bursted Manor Riding Centre (Area 11)
Rebecca Tombs, Pett Bottom, Near Bridge, Canterbury, CT4 6EH, United Kingdom
01227 830568
burstedmanor@gmail.com

Cabin Equestrian Centre (Area 1)
Fiona Quennell, Ordiefauld, Keithhall, Inverurie, AB51 0LL, United Kingdom
01467 624378
cabinecpc@gmail.com

Caistor Equestrian Centre (Area 6)
Fiona Lundy, Moor Lane, Caistor, LN7 6SD, United Kingdom
01472 859341
info@caistorequestriancentre.com

Calvert Trust Pony Club Centre (Area 2)
Henri Carew, The Lake District Calvert Trust Riding Centre, Old Windebrowe, Keswick, CA12 4NT, United Kingdom
01768 772250
stables@calvertlakes.org.uk

Cantref Pony Club Centre (Area 10)
Mary Evans, Upper Cantref Farm, Cantref, Brecon, LD3 8LR, United Kingdom
01874 665223
riding@cantref.com

Cardiff Riding School (Area 10)
Cardiff City Council, Pontcanna Fields, Llandaff, CF5 2AX, United Kingdom
02920 383908
cardiffridingschool@cardiff.gov.uk

Casterton Sedbergh Prep School (Area 4)
Diane Hull, Kirkby Lonsdale, Carnforth, LA6 2SG, United Kingdom
01524 279200
diane.hull@sedberghprep.org

Castle View Stables (Area 1)
Ashleigh Campbell, Old Wick, Wick, Caithness, KW1 5TP, United Kingdom
07716 596164
ashleigholdwick@yahoo.co.uk

Catherington Equestrian Centre (Area 13)
Angeline Othen,187 Catherington lane, Catherington, PO8 0TB, United Kingdom
02392 596120
Catherington.ec@gmail.com

Cefngranod Stables (Area 18)
Dawn Hodson, Sarnau, Llandysul, SA44 6QB, United Kingdom
01239 654314
d.hodson@rocketmail.com

Cheshire Riding School (Area 5)
Andrea Foden, Cogshall Lane, Comberbach Northwich, CW9 6BS, United Kingdom
01606 892111
info@cheshireridingschool.co.uk

Chestnut Farm Stables (Area 6)
Debi Varley, Chestnut Farm, Hallaton Road, East Norton, LE7 9XF, United Kingdom
01858 555822
brookam@hotmail.com

Church Farm Equestrian Centre (Area 14)
Kay Padfield, Church Farm Stables, Charlton Road, BS31 2SL, United Kingdom
07787 561469
churchfarmec@outlook.com

Cimla Trekking and Equestrian Centre (Area 18)
Alistair Parker, Hawdref Ganol, Cimla, Neath SA12 9SL, United Kingdom
01639 644944
CimlaEquestrian@outlook.com

City of Derry Equestrian Centre (Area 17)
Pauline Lusby,30 Bigwood Road, Ardmore, BT47 3RP, United Kingdom
07850 208656
info@cityofderryequestrian.com

Cliffhollins Riding School (Area 3)
Angela Gardner, Cliffhollins Lane, East Bierley Bradford, BD4 6RQ, United Kingdom
01274 651386
info@cliffhollins.co.uk

Clyne Farm Centre (Area 18)
Geoff Haden, Clyne Farm Centre, Westport Avenue, Mayals, SA3 5AR, United Kingdom
01792 403333
hello@clynefarm.com

Coker Brown School of Riding (Area 16)
Charlotte Coker Brown,14 Fairview Road, Denbury, Newton Abbot, TQ12 6ET, United Kingdom
07967 472097
charlottecoker-brown@hotmail.com

Coleg Cambria (Area 5)
Karen Jones, Northop Campus, Mold Road, CH7 6AA, United Kingdom
01978 267401
pippa.norman@cambria.ac.uk

Coloured Cob Equestrian Centre (Area 6)
Sharon Tolley, Bank House Farm, Mansfield Road, Creswell, S80 4AA, United Kingdom
01909 725251
sales@colouredcob.co.uk

Comeytrowe Equestrian Centre (Area 15)
Janet Neeld, Higher Comeytrowe Farm, Comeytrowe, Taunton, TA4 1EQ, United Kingdom
01823 461385
ponyclub@comeytrowe.co.uk

Conwy Community Riding Centre (Area 5)
Wendy Tobias-Jones, Tanrallt Farm, Henryd, LL32 8EZ, United Kingdom
07840 871197
gwentj@btinternet.com

Corner Farm Equestrian (Area 7)
Lucy Johnson, Corner Farm Equestrian Centre, Painsbrook Lane, Hadnall, Shrewsbury, SY4 4BD, United Kingdom
01939 270944
lucy_k_johnson@hotmail.com

Cornilo Riding (Area 11)
Marina Aunger, The Stables, Sutton Court Farm, Sutton by Dover, CT15 5DF, United Kingdom
01304 380369
marinaaunger5@gmail.com

Coton House Farm Stables (Area 7)
Helen Wakefield-Martin,.Vicarage Lane, Whitington, Near Lichfield, WS14 9LQ, United Kingdom
01543 432429
martindarr7@aol.com

Cotswold Riding (Area 9)
Pat Haine, Upper Woodhills Farm, Lower Lemington, Moreton-in-Marsh, GL56 9NW, United Kingdom
07508 773255
info@cotswoldriding.com

Cottagers Plot Equestrian Centre (Area 6)
Sophie Brown, Cottagers Plot, Laceby, Grimsby, DN37 7DX, United Kingdom
01472 276427
sophiebrown344@hotmail.com

Country Treks (Area 7)
Steph Eddies-Davies, Ginny Hole, Green Lane, Stottesdon, Kidderminster, DY14 8US, United Kingdom
07388 786394
enquiries@horsetreks.co.uk

Courses for Horses (Area 7)
Mary Stitson, Lower Stonehouse Farm, Brown Edge, Stoke on Trent, ST6 8TF, United Kingdom
01782 505664
admin@coursesforhorses.org.uk

Coventry and District Pony Club (Area 7)
Sandy Sandon, Anker Cottage Farm, Caldecote, Nuneaton, CV10 0TN, United Kingdom
02476383103
sandysandon@btconnect.com

Cranleigh School Equestrian Centre (Area 13)
Cranleigh School, Horseshoe Lane, Cranleigh, GU6 8QQ, United Kingdom
01483 276426
stables@cranleigh.org

Croft Riding Centre Pony Club (Area 4)
Clare Broughton, Spring Lane, Croft, Warrington, WA3 7AS, United Kingdom
01925 763715
info@croftridingcentre.co.uk

Cuckoo Riding Centre (Area 11)
Gaynor Lawrence, Palstre Court Road, Wittersham, TN30 7PX, United Kingdom
07771962524
mememia81@aol.com

Currypool Equestrian (Area 15)
Elaine Foster,109 Swang Cottage, Currypool, Cannington, TA5 2NH, United Kingdom
07835 579960
currypoolequestrian@outlook.com

Daisy Bank Farm (Area 5)
Julie Wilson, Clay Hill Lane, Queensferry, CH5 2AQ, United Kingdom
07808 986936
julie@daisy-bank-farm.co.uk

Dam Top Riding Centre (Area 4)
Judith Weymont, Dam Top Farm, Rossendale, BB4 7PZ, United Kingdom
01706 221024
garth.weymont@btinternet.com

Dark Deer Croft (Area 1)
Siobhan Thomson, Millness, Glen Urquhart, IV63 6TW, United Kingdom
01456 476201
info@darkdeer.co.uk

Darlington Stables (Area 4)
Janet Reid, Hooter Hall, Elton Lane, Winterley, CW11 4TJ, United Kingdom
01270759319
darlington.stables@hotmail.com

Deandane Riding Stables (Area 4)
Martin Whalley, Gathurst Road, Shevington, Wigan, WN6 8JB, United Kingdom
01257 252086
deandane@btinternet.com

Deanswood Equestrian Centre (Area 8)
Sarah Dean, Cressing Park, Braintree Road, Cressing, CM77 8JB, United Kingdom
01376 560522
shareteam@hotmail.co.uk

Deen City Farm (Area 11)
Joanna Henbrey,39 Windsor Avenue, London, SW19 2RR, United Kingdom
020 853 5858
stables1@deencityfarm.co.uk

Deepdene Riding Stables (Area 11)
Chelsea Donovan, Badlesmere, Ashford Road, Faversham, ME13 0NZ, United Kingdom
01233 740228
deepdenestables@gmail.com

Defence Academy Saddle Club (Area 9)
Tina Starling, Defence Academy of The United Kingdom, Shrivenham, Swindon, SN6 8LA, United Kingdom
01793 785489
ssponyclub19@gmail.com

Dinefwr Riding Centre (Area 18)
Penny Jenner, Llandyfan, Ammanford, SA18 2UD, United Kingdom
01269 850042
dinefwrriding@btconnect.com

Dovecote Farm Equestrian Centre (Area 6)
Heather Gunn, Dovecote Farm, Orston, NG13 9NS, United Kingdom
01949 851204
dovecotefarm@hotmail.com

Drakes Farm Riding School (Area 15)
Chris Mattravers, Church Road, Ilton, Ilminster, TA19 9EY, United Kingdom
01460 929 766
email@drakesfarm.co.uk

Ealing Riding School (Area 12)
Ailean Mills, Ealing Riding School, 17-19 Gunnersbury Avenue, London, W5 3XD, United Kingdom
02089923808
ealingponyclub@gmail.com

East Lodge Farm Equestrian Centre (Area 7)
Thomas White, East Lodge Farm, Washbrook Lane, Ecton, Northampton, NN6 0QU, United Kingdom
01604 810244
eastlodgefarmequestriancentre@outlook.com

Ebborlands Riding Centre (Area 14)
Eileen Gibbs, Wookey Hole, Wells, BA5 1AY, United Kingdom
01749 672550
eileen.gibbs1@btinternet.com

Ebony Horse Club (Area 11)
Naomi Howgate, Ebony Horse Club, 51 Millbrook Road, Brixton, SW9 7JD, United Kingdom
02077383478
info@ebonyhorseclub.org

Eccleston Equestrian Centre (Area 4)
Karen Norris, Ulnes Walton Lane, Leyland, Preston, PR26 8LT, United Kingdom
01772 600093
karen@equestrian-northwest.co.uk

Echos Equestrian (Area 12)
Lauren Dawes, Slough Road, Iver Heath, SL0 0DZ, United Kingdom
01895 347186
lauren@echosequestrian.co.uk

Equestrian at Coworth Park (Area 13)
Katelyn Winter, Coworth Park Hotel, Blacknest Road, Sunninghill, Ascot, SL5 7SE, United Kingdom
01344 756763 / 07584
equestrian.cpa@dorchestercollection.com

Equine Learning (Area 7)
Nicola Hepburn, Wootton Park Farm, Alcester Road, Wootton Wawen, Henley in Arden, B95 6HJ, United Kingdom
01564 642101
info@equinelearning.org.uk

Eston Equitation Centre (Area 2)
Laura Storey, Villa Marie, Occupation Road, Eston, Middlesbrough, TS6 9HA, United Kingdom
01642 452260
info@estonequitation.com

Evergreen Stables (Area 12)
Rachel Billing, Billings Brook Farm, Wrights Lane, Gayton, NN7 3ES, United Kingdom
01604 858247
billingsbrookstables@gmail.com

Faughanvale Stables (Area 17)
Patricia Dalton,11 Dunlade Road, Greysteel, BT47 3EF, United Kingdom
02871 811843
valestables@hotmail.co.uk

Featherbed Stables (Area 7)
Donna Brookes, Featherbed Lane, Wilmcote, CV37 9UQ, United Kingdom
07399156942
donnawillis6@googlemail.com

Fergushill Riding Stables (Area 19)
Gillian Beattie, Broomhill Farm, Fergushill, Kilwinning, KA13 7RF, United Kingdom
07842 166799
cevara@btinternet.com

Field House Equestrian Centre (Area 2)
Rebekah Reay, Fieldhouse Farm, Howden Le Wear, Crook, DL15 8EE, United Kingdom
01388 766687
rebekahreay@live.co.uk

Finchale View Riding School (Area 2)
Susan Mordey, Pitt House Lane, Leamside, DH4 6QR, United Kingdom
07761 642435
finchaleview@gmail.com

Fir Tree Farm Equestrian Centre Ltd (Area 2)
Katherine Waugh, Fir Tree Farm, Forest Hall, Newcastle, NE12 7PS, United Kingdom
07401 755062
firtreefarmridingschool@yahoo.co.uk

Fletchers Farm Riding School (Area 8)
Emily Bradshaw, Fletchers Farm, Rams Farm Road, Fordham, Colchester, CO6 3NT, United Kingdom
01206 242210
manager@fletchersfarm.co.uk

Folly Farm Equestrian Centre (Area 6)
Rebecca Hardy,25 London Road, Yaxley, Peterborough, PE7 3NQ, United Kingdom
01733 242783
folly.farm@yahoo.co.uk

Fordbank Equi Centre (Area 19)
Fiona Ferguson, Fairydale Cottage, Beith Road, PA10 2NS, United Kingdom
07572 424692
feefee42@live.co.uk

Fort Widley Equestrian Centre (Area 13)
Portsdown Hill Road, Cosham, Portsmouth, PO6 3LS, United Kingdom
02392 324553
equestrian@peterashleyactivitycentres.co.uk

Four Winds Equestrian Centre (Area 6)
Paula Leverton, Leaveslake Drove, West Pinchbeck, Spalding, PE11 3QJ, United Kingdom
01775 640533
paula@fourwindsequestrian.co.uk

Foxcote House Riding School (Area 9)
Sarah Everitt, Foxcote House, Foxcote, GL54 4LW, United Kingdom
01242 820663
sarah.everitt@live.com

Foxhills Riding Centre (Area 7)
David Blake, Bridle Lane, Walsall, WS9 0RG, United Kingdom
01213 609160
info@mygg.co.uk

Free Spirit Equestrian (Area 17)
L Hutchinson,41 Maytown Road, Bessbrook, Newry, BT35 7NE, United Kingdom
07775 724667
freespiritequestrian@hotmail.co.uk

Friars Hill Stables (Area 3)
Alison Brown, Friars Hill, Sinnington, York, YO62 6SL, United Kingdom
01751 432758
friarshillridingstables@gmail.com

Galgorm Parks Riding School (Area 17)
Sara Kyle,112 Sand Road, Ballymena, BT42 1D
United Kingdom
02825 880269
sara.r.kyle@gmail.com

Ghyll Park Equestrian (Area 11)
Sally-Ann Dale, Farmside, Lake Street, Mark Cross, Crowborough, TN6 3NT, United Kingdom
07974638536
sally@ghyllparkequestrian.co.uk

Gillians Riding School Pony Club Centre (Area 8)
Gillian Head, Brayside Farm, Clay Hill, Enfiel
EN2 9JL, United Kingdom
020 8366 5445
gilliansridingschool@outlook.com

Glen Tanar Equestrian Centre (Area 1)
Jacqueline Riley, The Stables, Glen Tanar, Aboyne, AB34 5EU, United Kingdom
01339 886448
gtec.t21@btinternet.com

Gleneagles Equestrian Centre (Area 1)
Gleneagles Hotel, The Equestrian School, Th
Gleneagles Hotel, Auchterarder, PH3 1NF, United Kingdom
01764 694344
equestrian@gleneagles.com

Gleneagles Equestrian Centre (Area 13)
Deborah Day, Allington Lane, West End, Southampton, SO30 3HQ, United Kingdom
02380 473370 / 07796
info@gleneagles.org.uk

Gorswen Riding School (Area 5)
Ken Jones, Pentre Felin, Plas Road, Holyhead, LL65 2LY, United Kingdom
07780 767941
rthowen@gmail.com

Goulds Green Riding School (Area 12)
Gail Jupp, The Stables, Goulds Green, Hillingdon, UB8 3DG, United Kingdom
01895 446256
sales@gouldsgreenridingschool.co.uk

Grafton Farm Riding Centre Ltd (Area 7)
Bockleton, Tenbury Wells, WR15 8PT, United Kingdom
01568 750602
grafton.farm@btinternet.com

Greatham Equestrian Centre (Area 13)
Debbie Roche, Springwood Stables, Longmoor Road, Greatham, GU33 6AH, United Kingdom
01420 538810
info@greathamequestriancentre.co.uk

Green Farm Riding Stables (Area 18)
Zana Llewellyn, The Green, Trebanos, Pontardawe, Swansea, SA8 4BR, United Kingdom
01792 862947
l.zana@yahoo.co.uk

Green Meadow Riding Centre (Area 10)
Judith England, Dare Valley Country Park, Aberdare, CF44 7PT, United Kingdom
01685 874961
judith.england@btconnect.com

Greenways Stables Ltd (Area 13)
Sally Blackmore, Lower Eashing, Godalming, GU7 2QF, United Kingdom
07442530080
info@greenways-stables.co.uk

Grenaby Estates Limited (Area 4)
Joanne Crookall, Grenaby Mooar, Grenaby, Malew, IM9 3BD, United Kingdom
01624 829565
yard@grenabyestates.com

Grenoside Equestrian Centre Ltd (Area 3)
Zoe Smith, Barnes Green, Penistone Road, Grenoside, Sheffield, S35 8NA, United Kingdom
01142 402548
hello@grenoside-equestrian.co.uk

Grove Farm Riding School (Area 11)
Louise Mathews, Grove Lane, Iden, Nr Rye, TN31 7PX, United Kingdom
01797 280362
grovefarm.rs@hotmail.co.uk

Grove House Stables Pony Club Centre (Area 6)
Andrew Stennett, Grove House Stables Equestrian Centre, Grovewood Road, Misterton, Doncaster, DN10 4EF, United Kingdom
01427 890802
ghs1991@grovehousestables.co.uk

Gym-Khana Club at Valley Farm (Area 8)
Phoebe Ling, Valley Farm Equestrian Leisure, Valley Farm, Wickham Market, Woodbridge, IP13 0ND, United Kingdom
01728 746916
phoebe@valleyfarm.co.uk

Hall Farm Stables (Area 8)
Tessa Frost, Cambridge Road, Waterbeach, CB25 9NJ, United Kingdom
01223 860087
enquiries@hallfarmstables.com

Hanford School (Area 14)
Rory Johnson, Hanford School, Child Okeford, Blandford Forum, DT11 8HN, United Kingdom
01258 860219
pearsonc@hanfordschool.co.uk

Hargate Equestrian (Area 6)
Carol Smith, Egginton Road, Hilton, DE65 5FJ, United Kingdom
01283 730606
info@hargateequestrian.co.uk

Hargate Hill Equestrian Centre (Area 4)
Jenna Tyldesley, Hargate Hill, Glossop, SK13 6JL, United Kingdom
01457 865518
enquiries@hargatehill.com

Havard Stables (Area 18)
Hannah McLoughlin, Havard Stables, Dinas Cross, Newport, SA42 0SR, United Kingdom
07968 647762
havardstables@live.co.uk

Hayfield EC (Area 1)
John Crawford, Hazelhead Park, Aberdeen, AB15 8BB, United Kingdom
01224 315703
info@hayfield.com

Hemsted Forest Equestrian Centre (Area 11)
Kerry Hobbs, Golford Road, Benenden, TN17 4AJ, United Kingdom
01580 240086
kerryhobbs@outlook.com

Hewshott Farm Stables (Area 13)
Caroline Ewen, Hewshott Lane, Liphook, GU30 7SU, United Kingdom
07721 650758
info@hewshottfarmstables.co.uk

Highcross Equestrian Centre (Area 7)
Vivien Twiggs, High Cross, Claybrooke Magna, LE17 5AZ, United Kingdom
01455 202449
highcrossec@aol.com

Hill Farm Equestrian Centre (Area 8)
Hazel Ackland, Stonewold, Hill Farm Lane, Chelmondiston, IP9 1JU, United Kingdom
01473 780406
hillfarmec@hotmail.co.uk

Hill Farm Riding Stables and Pony Club Centre (IoW) (Area 13)
Jayne Brown, Hill Lane, Freshwater, PO40 9T United Kingdom
07748 253899
hillfarmstablesiow@gmail.com

Hill Farm Stables and Livery Yard (Area 8)
Sarah Moorbey, Ashfields Road, Elmswell, IP3 9HL, United Kingdom
07845 320424
hillfarmridingschool@yahoo.com

Hill House School Pony Club (Area 6)
D Holland, Hill House School, Sixth Avenue, Doncaster Finningley Airport, Doncaster, DN 3GG, United Kingdom
01302 776300
info@hillhouse.doncaster.sch.uk

Hilltop Equestrian Centre (Area 8)
Sharon Newbound,180 High Street, Yelling, PE19 6SD, United Kingdom
01480 880232
ann@mariemalone.plus.com

Hole Farm Trekking Centre (Area 7)
Carol Jones,36 Watery Lane, Quinton, Birmingham, B32 3BS, United Kingdom
0121 422 3464
cjones60@sky.com

Hollyoaks Riding (Area 13)
Lucy Gregory, Manningshill, Horseshoe Lane, Cranleigh, GU6 8QN, United Kingdom
07881 543697
lucyrosegregory@aol.co.uk

Holt's Equestrian Centre (Area 4)
Anne-Margaret Holt, Dry Gap Farm, Bury Old Road, Ramsbottom, Bury, BL0 0RX, United Kingdom
07717527399
holt-equestrian@hotmail.co.uk

Hooks Cross Equestrian (Area 8)
Ruth Davies, Oaks Cross Farm, Hooks Cross, Watton-at-Stone, SG14 3RY, United Kingdom
01920 438240
hookscrossequestrian@gmail.com

Horseshoes Riding School (Area 11)
Ros Hargreaves, Dean Street, East Farleigh, Maidstone, ME15 0PR, United Kingdom
01622 746161
horseshoesridingschool@hotmail.co.uk

Hot to Trot School of Equitation (Area 8)
Hannah Vincent,148 Bunwell Street, Bunwell, Norwich, NR16 1QY, United Kingdom
01379 677679
info@hottotrotschoolofequitation.co.uk

Hundleby Riding Centre (Area 6)
Russell Lovatt, Sumpter Farm, North Beck Lane, Hundleby, PE23 5NB, United Kingdom
07584 047340
slequinejournalism@gmail.com

Huntersfield Equestrian Centre (Area 9)
Nico Van den Berg, Petwick Farm, Challow, Faringdon, SN7 8NT, United Kingdom
07729 680573
nico@huntersfieldec.com

Hunterswood Riding and Livery Stables (Area 16)
Christine Weeks, Yeoford, Crediton, EX17 5ET, United Kingdom
01363 772594
c.c.weeks@icloud.com

Iken Bay Riding (Area 8)
Lisa Kelly, Iken Road, Tunstal, Woodbridge, IP12 2EP, United Kingdom
01728 689065
kelly.lisa@hotmail.co.uk

Inadown Farm Livery Stables (Area 13)
F Janson, Newton Valence, Alton, GU34 3RR, United Kingdom
01420 588439
inadown@yahoo.co.uk

Island Magee Riding Centre (Area 17)
Barbara McCluskey,103 Brownsbay Road, Island Magee, Larne, BT40 3TL, United Kingdom
02893 382108
marymcly44@hotmail.co.uk

Island Riding Centre (Area 13)
Louise Buckner, Staplers Road, Newport, PO30 2NB, United Kingdom
info@islandriding.com

K A Horses (Area 7)
Kerry Davies, The Lake House, Turley Green, Bridgnorth, WV15 6LR, United Kingdom
07919 484727
enquiries@kahorses.co.uk

Kays Equestrian (Area 17)
Michaela McFarland, Kilsmallon, Lack, BT93 0BR, United Kingdom
028 68 633178
kaysequestrian@hotmail.co.uk

Kent College Equine Unit (Area 11)
Lisa Miller, Kent College Farm, Moat Lane, Rough Common, Canterbury, CT2 9DR, United Kingdom
07807 093285
lmiller@kentcollege.co.uk

Kiln Stables Riding School (Area 13)
Angela Macleod, The Old Kiln Farm, Farnham Road, GU10 4JZ, United Kingdom
01420 520005
kilnstables@aol.com

Kilnsey Trekking and Riding Centre (Area 4)
Jane Pighills, The Homestead, Conistone with Kilnsey, Skipton, BD23 5HS, United Kingdom
01756 752861
janepighills@btinternet.com

Kimblewick Equestrian Centre (Area 8)
Sarah Moore, Low Road, North Tuddenham, Dereham, NR20 3HF, United Kingdom
07856 266990
nikkita@kimblewick.co.uk

Kingsmead Equestrian Centre (Area 11)
Fiona Tothill, Kingswood Lane, Hamsey Green, Warlingham, CR6 9AB, United Kingdom
07702 966102
kingsmead_horses@btinternet.com

Kingston Maurward College (Area 14)
Tamsyn Hannam, Manor Stables, Kingston Maurward College, Dorchester, DT2 8PY, United Kingdom
01305 215 063
manor.stables@kmc.ac.uk

Kingston Riding Centre (Area 11)
Lynne Mastroianni,38 Crescent Road, Kingston upon Thames, KT2 7RG, United Kingdom
020 8546 6361
kingston.r.c@btconnect.com

Knighton House School (Area 14)
Jacqui Bolt, Durweston, Blandford Forum, DT11 0PY, United Kingdom
01258 489186
jbolt@knightonhouse.co.uk

Knowle Hill Equestrian (Area 6)
H Stanton, Knowle Hill Farm, Ticknall, DE73 7JQ, United Kingdom
01332 862044
knowlehillequestrian@gmail.com

La Rocco Riding School (Area 16)
Lisa Dubois, Pennybrook Farm, Lower Newlands, Bradworthy, EX22 7RN, United Kingdom
01409 240166
ssalisbury462@btinternet.com

Lakefield Equestrian Centre (Area 16)
Becky Monk, Lower Pendavey Farm, Camelford, PL32 9TX, United Kingdom
01840 213279
lakefieldequestriancentre@btconnect.com

Lancing Equestrian (Area 11)
Jan Tupper, Hoe, Hoe Court, BN15 0QX, Unit Kingdom
01903 763815
jan@lancingequestrian.co.uk

Landlords Farm Equestrian Centre (Area
Michelle Pendlebury, Dicconson Lane, Aspu Wigan, WN2 1QD, United Kingdom
01942 831329
michellependlebury@hotmail.co.uk

Lands End Equestrian Centre (Area 13)
Suzy Jones, Whistley Mill Lane, Twyford, Reading, RG10 0RA, United Kingdom
07834 838111
info@landsendequestriancentre.com

Langtoft Stables (Area 6)
Carolyne Lister, Langtoft Fen, Peterborough PE6 9NX, United Kingdom
07703 743159
langstables@hotmail.co.uk

Larkrigg Riding School (Area 4)
Anne Wilson, Natland, Nr Kendal, LA9 7QS, United Kingdom
01539 560245
larkrigg@hotmail.co.uk

Lauras Lessons (Area 16)
Laura Axford, West Brendon Stables, Sutcombe, Holsworthy, EX22 7QW, United Kingdom
07480 646508
lauraslessons@hotmail.co.uk

Laurel View Equestrian Centre (Area 17)
Linda Davis,18 Knowehead Road, Templepatrick, Ballyclare, BT39 0BX, United Kingdom
02890 830649
laurelview01@btinternet.com

Lavant Equestrian (Area 13)
Lucy Thomson, Lavant Equestrian LLP, West Lavant, Chichester, PO18 9AH, United Kingdom
01243 530460
h.ingram@lavanteqestrian.co.uk

Lee Valley Riding Centre (Area 8)
Rachel Seddon,71 Leabridge Road, Leyton, E10 7QL, United Kingdom
020 8556 2629
riding@leevalleypark.org.uk

Liege Manor Equestrian (Area 10)
Sarah Bassett, Liege Manor, Bonvilston, CF5 6TQ, United Kingdom
01446 781648
liegemanor@btconnect.com

Lime Oaks Equestrian Centre (Area 3)
Heather Talbot, Woodhall, Selby, YO8 6TG, United Kingdom
07709 781858
heathertalbot58@gmail.com

Little Brook Equestrian (Area 11)
Sally O'Neill, East Park Lane, Newchapel, Near Lingfield, RH7 6HS, United Kingdom
01342 837546
sally@littlebrookequestrian.co.uk

Little Margate Equestrian (Area 16)
Rachel Philpott, Little Margate Farm, Margate Lane, Bodmin, PL30 4AL, United Kingdom
07917 762102
info@littlemargateequestrian.com

Little Wratting Riding School (Area 8)
Tayla Trowbridge, Littlecourt, Haverhill Road, Little Wratting, CB9 7UD, United Kingdom
07507647188
taylatrowbridge@btinternet.com

Littlebourne Equestrian Centre (Area 12)
Caroline Dent, Littlebourne Farm, Northwood Road, Harefield, UB9 6PU, United Kingdom
01895 824350
info@littlebournefarm.com

Llannerch Equestrian Centre (Area 5)
Sian Gresley Jones, Llanerch EC, St Asaph, LL17 0BD, United Kingdom
01745 730199
siangj@btinternet.com

Lodge Equine Stables (Area 17)
Lesley Johnston,10 Ballyloughan Road, Richhill, BT61 9ND, United Kingdom
02838 870359
lesleyjohnston20@gmail.com

Lodge Farm Equestrian Centre (Area 7)
Ken and Mrs Christina Carr, Off Mill Lane, Wetley Rocks, Stoke on Trent, ST9 0BN, United Kingdom
01782 551961
info@lodgefarmriding.co.uk

Lodge Riding Centre (Area 4)
Sue Blong, Dacres Bridge Lane, Tarbock, L35 1QZ, United Kingdom
0151 489 8886
orry.king@btinternet.com

Long Lane Equestrian (Area 6)
Sally Warwick, Long Lane, Kegworth, DE74 2GA, United Kingdom
01509 674655 / 07941
longlane.equestrian@hotmail.com

Longfield Equestrian Centre (Area 4)
Christine Farnaby, Middle Longfield Farm, Long Hey Lane, Todmorden, OL14 6JN, United Kingdom
01706 812736
info@longfieldequestriancentre.co.uk

Lower Farm Stables (Area 11)
Jane Brown and Helen Lewin,71 Stoke Road, Stoke D Abernon, KT11 3PU, United Kingdom
01932 867545
enquiries@lowerfarmstables.com

Lower Tokenbury Equestrian Centre (Area 16)
Richard Lucas, Lower Tokenbury Farm, Upton Cross, Liskeard, PL14 5AR, United Kingdom
07880 702704
tokenburyriding@hotmail.co.uk

Lucton School (Area 10)
Emma Coates, Lucton School, Lucton, Leominster, HR6 9PN, United Kingdom
01568 782000
enquiries@luctonschool.org

Lychgate Farm Equestrian LLP (Area 7)
Jane Brown, Lychgate Farm Equestrian LLP, Lychgate Lane, Burbage, Hinckley, LE10 2DS, United Kingdom
01455 632188
lychgatefarm@gmail.com

Malvern Riding School (Area 9)
Julie Davies-Bennetts, Northend Farm House, Northend Lane, Malvern, WR13 5AD, United Kingdom
07766 853668
handsonhorses@btinternet.com

Manchester Pony Club Centre (Area 4)
Damon Atkinson, Wythenshawe Park Riding Stables, Wythenshawe Park, Wythenshawe Road, M23 0AB, United Kingdom
07876 555528
Info@wythenshaweparkridingstables.co.uk

Marros Riding Centre (Area 18)
Hazel Smith, Marros, Pendine, SA33 4PN, United Kingdom
01994 453777
info@marros-farm.co.uk

Meadow School of Riding (Area 6)
Dawn Whitmore-Kirby, Bowleys Barn Farm, Stanford Lane, Normanton on Soar, LE12 5ER, United Kingdom
01509 891690
dawnwhitmore@hotmail.com

Meadow View Stables (Area 3)
Gayle Dunleavy, Cow Hill Gate Lane, Illingworth, HX2 9PB, United Kingdom
07793 324761
meadowviewst@gmail.com

Mere Lane Equestrian Centre (Area 6)
P Whitaker, Mere Lane, Oadby, LE2 4SA, United Kingdom
01162 710122
merelane1@gmail.com

Middleton Park Equestrian Centre (Area 3)
Anna Burke, Middleton Grove, Leeds, LS11 5TZ United Kingdom
0113 277 1962
info@mpec-rda.co.uk

Midgeland Riding School (Area 4)
Wendy Ellis,460 Midgeland Road, Marton Moss, Blackpool, FY4 5EE, United Kingdom
01253 693312
midgeland@hotmail.co.uk

Mierscourt Valley Riding School (Area 11)
Nadia Cooke, Mierscourt Road, Rainham, Gillingham, ME8 8PH, United Kingdom
07736 454388
mvridingschool@yahoo.co.uk

Mill House (Area 6)
Anna Walker, Mill Lane, Belton, Loughborough, LE12 9UJ, United Kingdom
07968 118850
annacbaxter@aol.com

Moat Farm Riding Centre (Area 8)
Patricia Adams, Moat Farm, Golden Lane, Lawshall, Bury St Edmunds, IP29 4PS, United Kingdom
01284 830098
tish@moat-farm.co.uk

Moor Farm Stables (Area 7)
Elizabeth White, Wall Hill Road, Corley Moor, Coventry, CV7 8AP, United Kingdom
01676 540594
liz@mfstables.co.uk

Moor Hall Farm Polo Centre (Area 8)
Alec Banner Eve, Moor Hall Farm, Harlow Tye, Harlow CM17 0PE
07736060200
team@mhfpolo.com

Moorview Equestrian Centre (Area 4)
Ursula Dalton, Blacksnape Road, Blacksnape, Darwen, BB3 3PP, United Kingdom
01254 701557
moorviewreception@yahoo.co.uk

Mount Mascal Stables (Area 11)
Alison Window, Vicarage Road, Bexley, DA5 2AW, United Kingdom
020 8300 3947
office@mountmascalstables.com

Mousley House Farm Equestrian Centre (Area 7)
Victoria Woods, Case Lane, Hatton, CV35 7JG, United Kingdom
07395118782
mousleyhouseequestrian@outlook.com

Murton Equestrian Centre (Area 2)
Leigh Belbin, The Bridle, Murton Village, Shiremoor, Newcastle upon Tyne, NE27 0QD, United Kingdom
0191 257 1369
murtonequestriancentre@gmail.com

Mutterton Equine (Area 15)
Jo Palmer, Mutterton Cottage, Cullompton, EX15 1RL, United Kingdom
07795 664498
info@muttertonequine.com

Naburn Grange Riding Centre (Area 3)
Della Horn, York Road, Naburn, York, YO19 4RU, United Kingdom
01904 728283
brionyh10@hotmail.com

Nelson Park Riding Centre (Area 11)
Sarah Catterall, St Margarets Road, Woodchurch, Birchington, CT7 0HJ, United Kingdom
01843 822251
nelsonparkridingcentre@googlemail.com

Nether Hall Riding School (Area 3)
Adele Clayton,225 Rawthorpe Lane, Dalton, Huddersfield, HD5 9PD, United Kingdom
01484 431173
e11aea@hotmail.com

New Hill House (Area 4)
Danielle Perez, New Hill House Farm, Wood Lane, Great Altcar, L37 9BQ, United Kingdom
07590 455404
danielleperez@hotmail.co.uk

Newark Equestrian (Area 6)
Christine Carlile, Coddington Lane, Balderton, Newark, NG24 3NB, United Kingdom
07714 182876
refoster@talktalk.net

Newton Equestrian (Area 16)
Jemma Cattran, Newton Farm, Mullion, Helston, TR12 7JF, United Kingdom
01326 240388
info@newton-equestrian.co.uk

Newton Ferrers Equus (Area 16)
Roger Harris, Newton Downs Farm, Newton Ferrers, PL8 1JA, United Kingdom
01752 872 807
leahfoxharris@gmail.com

Nightingale Farm and Stud (Area 11)
Jackie Goddard, Nightingale Farm, Whiteacre Lane, Waltham, Near Canterbury, CT4 5SR, United Kingdom
01227 700349
jackie@mannixstud.com

Noakes Farm Riding Centre (Area 9)
Sallie Barrett, Bredenbury, Bromyard, HR7 4SY, United Kingdom
01885 483467
noakesfarm@btconnect.com

North Manor Equestrian Centre (Area 8)
Valli Hayes, Main Road, Bramfield, Halesworth, IP19 9HT, United Kingdom
01986 784552
vallihayes@sky.com

Northbrook Equestrian Centre (Area 8)
Andrea Pavet-Golding, New Road, Offord Cluny, St Neots, PE19 5RP, United Kingdom
01480 812654
northbrookec@gmail.com

Northington Stud and Stables (Area 13)
Francesca Baring, Grange Park, Northington Road, SO24 9TG, United Kingdom
07970 717093
northingtonstudandstables@gmail.com

Nuneaton and North Warwickshire Equestrian Centre (Area 7)
Sandra Haddon, Valley Road, Galley Common, Nuneaton, CV10 9NJ, United Kingdom
02476 392397
sandra.haddon@nnwec.org.uk

Oakfield Farm Pony Club Centre (Area 6)
Karen Wint, Belper Road, Stanley Common, Ilkeston, DE7 6FP, United Kingdom
01159 305358
info@oakfieldfarm.co.uk

Oakhanger Riding and Pony Club Centre (Area 5)
Nathalie Ecclestone, Holmshaw Lane, Crewe, CW1 5XE, United Kingdom
01270 876311
oakhangerridingcentre@outlook.com

Oaklands Riding School (Area 15) (Area 15)
Jacky Newbery, Oaklands, Ball Farm Road, Alphington, Exeter, EX2 9JA, United Kingdom
01392 272105
jacky@newoakstud.co.uk

Old Bexley Stables Pony Club (Area 11)
Wendy Tucker, Stable Lane, Vicarage Road, Bexley, DA5 2AW, United Kingdom
01322 557745
oldbex@aol.com

Old Tiger Stables (Area 8)
Lorraine Webster,22A Northfield Road, Soha
Ely, CB7 5UF, United Kingdom
07887 637121
lorraine@oldtigerstables.co.uk

Oldmoor Farm Riding School (Area 6)
Katie Renn, Oldmoor Farm, Robinettes Lane
Babbington, NG16 2ST, United Kingdom
07729 529042
oldmoorfarmridingschool@sky.com

Orchard Farm Equestrian Centre (Area 6)
Jamie Blanchard, West End, Hogsthorpe, Ne
Skegness, PE24 5PA, United Kingdom
01754 872319
abby.zanelli@btinternet.com

Otterbourne Riding Centre (Area 14)
Caroline Jackson, Rue de Planel, Torteval, GY
0LX, United Kingdom
01481 263085
nicholas_jackson@hotmail.co.uk

Oxmardyke Equestrian Centre (Area 3)
Rachel Kirby, Field View House, Tongue Lane
Gilberdyke, HU15 2UY, United Kingdom
07961 104690
oecuk@outlook.com

P and R Equestrian Centre (Area 6)
Pearl Massey, The Paddocks, Claxy Bank, Friskney, PE22 8PN, United Kingdom
07545 813962
pearlmasseyis@aol.com

Park Farm Riding School (Area 11)
Anne Seymour, Park Road, Preston, Canterbury, CT3 1HD, United Kingdom
01227 728349
parkfarmriding@yahoo.co.uk

Park Hall Equestrian (Area 8)
Penny Townsend, Park Hall Farm, Park Hall Road, Somersham, Huntingdon, PE28 3HQ, United Kingdom
07594 449583
penny_townsend22@yahoo.co.uk

Park Lane Stables (Area 11)
Natalie O'Rourke, Park Lane, Teddington, TW11 0HY, United Kingdom
07584 253799
parklanestables@googlemail.com

Parklands Arena (Area 6)
Ruth Sampson, Parklands, Worksop Road, Aston, Sheffield, S26 2AD, United Kingdom
07798 700733
sampsonruth@gmail.com

Parkside Stables (Area 6)
Amanda Stalker, Wingfield Road, Alfreton, DE55 7AP, United Kingdom
01773 835193
parksidestables@btinternet.com

Parkview Riding School (Area 6)
B Rossi,100 Ansty Lane, Thurcaston, LE7 7JB, United Kingdom
0116 236 4858
charlie@parkviewridingschool.co.uk

Pathhead Equestrian Centre (Area 1)
Ali Bruce, Pathhead Farm, Forfar Road, Kirriemuir, DD8 5BY, United Kingdom
01575 572173
enquiries@pathhead.com

Pen Y Coed Riding Stables (Area 5)
James Hanson, Llynclys Hill, Oswestry, SY10 8LG, United Kingdom
01691 830608
penycoed.holidays@virgin.net

Petasfield Stables (Area 8)
Crissie Flemming, Mangrove Lane, Hertford, SG13 8QQ, United Kingdom
07775 931343
crissie@petasfieldstables.com

Pevlings Farm Riding and Livery Stables (Area 14)
Alison Tytheridge, Cabbage Lane, Horsington, Templecombe, BA8 0DA, United Kingdom
01963 370990
atytheridge@hotmail.co.uk

Pigeon House Equestrian (Area 9)
Sarah Hill, Pigeon House Lane, Church Hanborough, Witney, OX29 8AF, United Kingdom
01993 881628
schill2005@icloud.com

Pine Ridge Riding School (Area 11)
Jenny Butler-Smith, Pound Lane, Knockholt, TN14 7NE, United Kingdom
01959 533161
pineridgers@hotmail.com

Pony Grove (Area 13)
Hall Grove School, Hall Grove, London Road, Bagshot, GU19 5HZ, United Kingdom
07802766423
ponygrovelimited@gmail.com

Poplar Park Equestrian Centre (Area 8)
Antonia Hardwick, Hollesley, Woodbridge, IP12 3NA, United Kingdom
01394 411023
poplarpark@googlemail.com

Poppyfield Equestrian (Area 6)
Jo Morton, Branston Road, Heighington, Lincoln, LN4 1QQ, United Kingdom
01522 871788
jomorton@btinternet.com

Priory Stables (Area 18)
J Jones, Coed Season Farm, Pentre Road, Groves End, SA4 8DD, United Kingdom
07976 605106
leighton.rees@gmail.com

Putley Pony Club Centre (Area 9)
Sharon Pudge, Newtons Farm, Putley, Ledbury, HR8 2QW, United Kingdom
01531 670256
putleyhorseridingschool@outlook.com

QSR Equestrian Centre (Area 15)
Catherine Chester, Middle Halsway Farm, Crowcombe, Taunton, TA4 4BA, United Kingdom
01984 718732
thequantockschoolofriding@yahoo.co.uk

Quarry Farm Riding Stables (Area 11)
Rosie Langbridge, Quarry Farm, West Park Road, Lingfield, RH7 6HT, United Kingdom
07710 681494
officequarryfarm@gmail.com

Quob Stables Equestrian Centre (Area 13)
Beth Boyes, Durley Brook Road, Durley, Southampton, SO32 2AR, United Kingdom
02380 694657
enquiries@quobstables.com

Raby House Stables (Area 5)
Faye Bedford, Benty Heath Lane, Willaston, CH64 1SB, United Kingdom
07521 719031
rabyhousestables@gmail.com

Radway Riding School LLP (Area 7)
Maggie Boswell, Farnborough Road, Radway, CV35 0UN, United Kingdom
01295 670265
radwayridingschool@hotmail.com

RD Equestrian (Area 17)
Roisin Donnelly,126 Main Street, Fintona, BT78 2AE, United Kingdom
07709 846447
rd10@hotmail.co.uk

Red Park Equestrian Centre (Area 15)
Jill Martin, Egrove Way, Williton, TA4 4TB, United Kingdom
01984 632373
red.park@btinternet.com

Red Piece Equestrian Stables (Area 6)
Antonia McKinnon-Wood, Stanion Road, Brigstock, NN14 1DZ, United Kingdom
07854 323626
redpiecees@gmail.com

Regal Equestrian (Area 9)
Fran Bird, Green Lane Farm, Traitors' Ford Lane, Ascott, Shipston-on-Stour, CV36 5PP, United Kingdom
01608 684113
fran.bird@regalequestrian.co.uk

Rheidol Riding Centre (Area 18)
Iola Evans, Capel Bangor, Aberystwyth, SY23 4EL, United Kingdom
01970 880863
iola.evans@btinternet.com

Ridge Farm Riding School (Area 11)
Fiona McGuinness, Ridge Farm Cottage, Ridg Row, Acrise, Near Folkestone, CT18 8JT, Unitec Kingdom
01303 892222
ridgefarmridingschool@gmail.com

Ringer Villa Farm (Area 6)
Yvonne Evans, Ringer Lane, Clowne, S43 4BX United Kingdom
01246 810456
yvonne@new-direction.org.uk

Riverside Equestrian Centre (Area 3)
Michaela Preston, Heron Bank Farm, Bawtry Road, Tickhill, Doncaster, DN11 9EX, United Kingdom
01302 744499
riversideeqc@btinternet.com

Robin House Equestrian (Area 4)
Janet Webster, Robin House Lane, Briercliffe, Burnley, BB10 3RW, United Kingdom
07939 976368
janetwebster1@live.co.uk

Robinsons Equiteach (Area 2)
Claire Robinson, Tunstall Farm, Tunstall Lane, Middlesbrough, TS7 0NU, United Kingdom
07884 276031
claire.totrobinson82@btinternet.com

Rockstar Equine (Area 7)
Kay Scott-Jarvis, Cocksparrow Lane, Penkridge, WS12 4PB, United Kingdom
01543406021
kay.rockstarequitationcentre@gmail.com

Roman Bank Equestrian (Area 8)
Terri Herbert, Roman Bank, Walpole St Andrew, Near Wisbech, PE14 7JY, United Kingdom
01945 780179
rbepc@hotmail.com

Roocroft Riding Stables (Area 4)
Judith Burton, Barrons Farm, Courage Low Lane, Wrightington, Nr Wigan, WN6 9PJ, United Kingdom
01257 252225
judith_burton@hotmail.com

Rookery Team Pony Club (Area 7)
Natalie Burrows, Rookery Farm, Ettington, Stratford on Avon, CV37 7TN, United Kingdom
07973 133569
rookeryteampcc@gmail.com

Rookin House Farm (Area 2)
Deborah Hogg, Troutbeck, Penrith, CA11 0SS, United Kingdom
01768 483561
enquiries@rookinhouse.co.uk

Rosewall Equestrian (Area 14)
Mary Green, Mills Road, Osmington Mills, Weymouth, DT3 6HA, United Kingdom
01305 833578
riding@weymouthcamping.com

Royal Alexandra and Albert School RS (Area 11)
Irini Economou, Gatton park, Reigate, RH2 0TD, United Kingdom
01737 649069
stables@gatton-park.org.uk

Royal Armoured Corps Saddle Club (Area 14)
Stephanie Buchanan, RAC Saddle Club Office, Allenby Barracks, Bovington, Wareham, BH20 6JA, United Kingdom
01929 403 580
office@racsaddleclub.co.uk

Running Well Equestrian Centre (Area 8)
Ruth Dowie, Warren Road, Rettendon, Chelmsford, CM3 8DG, United Kingdom
01268711221
info@runningwell.co.uk

Russells Equestrian Centre (Area 13)
Carol Boulton, Russell Equestrian Centre, New Place, Allington Lane, West End, Southampton, SO30 3HQ, United Kingdom
02380 473693
veritytidmarsh@yahoo.co.uk

Rye Street Farm Equestrian Centre (Area 11)
Hannah Loveridge, Rye Street, Cliffe, Rochester, ME3 7UD, United Kingdom
01634 221030
rye.street@btinternet.com

Saddles Riding Centre (Area 11)
Carly Thomas, Stable Lane, Off Vicarage Road, Bexley, DA5 2AW, United Kingdom
01322 525219
saddlesrc@gmail.com

Sandridgebury Riding School (Area 12)
DT & CI Burrows, Sandridgebury Farm, Sandridgebury Lane, Sandridgebury, St. Albans, AL3 6JB, United Kingdom
01727 851952
office@sandridgeburyridingschool.co.uk

Sandroyd School (Area 14)
Frances Cattell,16 Morrison Avenue, Tisbury, Salisbury, SP3 6GX, United Kingdom
01725 516264
fcattell@sandroyd.com

Sawston Riding School (Area 8)
Fiona Rowe, Sawston Riding School, Common Lane, Sawston, Cambridge, CB22 3HW, United Kingdom
01223 835198
sawstonridingschool@live.co.uk

Scholland Equestrian at Kilconquhar (Area 1)
Debbie Maas, Kilconquhar Castle, Kilconquher, Leven, KY9 IEZ, United Kingdom
01333 340501
info@scholland.com

Scropton Riding and Driving Centre (Area 6)
Abbie Hall, Scropton RDA, Watery Lane, Scropton, DE65 5PL, United Kingdom
01283 812753
enquiries@scroptonequestrian.com

Seaview Riding School (Area 4)
Claire Hayton, Biggar Village, Walney Island, Barrow in Furness, LA14 3YG, United Kingdom
01229 474251
claireseaview@hotmail.co.uk

Severnvale Equestrian Centre (Area 10)
E Winter, Tidenham, Chepstow, NP16 7LL, United Kingdom
01291 623412
svec@clara.co.uk

Shardeloes Farm Equestrian Centre (Area 12)
Anthony Williams, Cherry Lane, Woodrow, Amersham, HP7 0QF, United Kingdom
01494 433333
office@shardeloesfarm.com

Shedfield Equestrian Centre (Area 13)
C Collins, Shedfield Equestrian Centre, Botle Road, Shedfield, Southampton, SO32 2HL, United Kingdom
01329 830387
shedfielderidingschool@gmail.com

Silvermere Equestrian Centre (Area 13)
Ken Spragg, Bramley Hedge Farm , Redhill Road, Cobham, KT11 1EQ, United Kingdom
01932 864040
enquiries@silvermere-equestrian.co.uk

Silverstone Riding Stables (Area 12)
Sophie Brennan, Blackmires Farm, Silversto Towcester, NN12 8UZ, United Kingdom
01327 857280
silverstoneriding@gmail.com

Simonswood Riding Academy (Area 4)
Lisa McHugh, Hall Lane, Simonswood, L33 4YQ, United Kingdom
01515 450538
lisa.mchugh@hotmail.com

Skye Trekking Centre (Area 1)
Stefi Duff, Suledale, Bernisdale, Portree, IV51 9PA, United Kingdom
01470 582419
skyetrekking@btconnect.com

SMS Equestrian (Area 14)
Sarah Mitchell Sheppard, The Stables, Greer Drove, Fovant, Salibury, SP3 5JG, United Kingdom
07843 603147
smsbookings@outlook.com

Smugglers Equestrian Centre (Area 10)
Melissa Rawlins-Burles, Pen-Deri Farm Lane Manmoel, Blackwood, NP12 0HU, United Kingdom
01495 226658
melissa@smugglers-ec.co.uk

Snowball Farm Equestrian Centre (Area 12)
Natalie Western-Kaye, Dorney Wood Road, Burnham, SL1 8EH, United Kingdom
01628 666222
office@snowballfarm.co.uk

Snowdon Farm Riding School (Area 6)
Cath Meehan, Snowdon Lane, Troway, Sheffield, S21 5RT, United Kingdom
01246 417172
cath.meehan@btconnect.com

Snowdonia Riding Stables (Area 5)
Melissa Hickey, Waunfawr, Caernarfon, Gwynedd, Snowdonia LL55 4PQ
01286 650342
info@snowdoniaridingstables.co.uk

Somerby Equestrian Centre (Area 6)
Gail Stimson, Newbold Lane, Somerby, LE14 2PP, United Kingdom
01664 454838
somerbyequestriancentre@hotmail.com

South Farm Riding Stables (Area 11)
June Spencer, Eagle Cottage, South Farm, Langton Green, TN3 9JN, United Kingdom
01892 864401
june.southfarm17@uwclub.net

Southborough Lane Stables (Area 11)
K D Jackson,321A Southborough Lane, Bromley, BR2 8BG, United Kingdom
0208 467 5236
jumpinggeegees@hotmail.com

Southview Equestrian Centre (Area 6)
Elizabeth Swift, London Road, Silk Willoughby, NG34 8RU, United Kingdom
01529 455676 - 07718 751405
rachel87emma@gmail.com

Springbank Riding School (Area 5)
Alisha Lamb, Spring Bank, Willymoor Lane, Tushingham, SY13 4QW, United Kingdom
07984 524573
sbridingschool@aol.com

Springhill Farm Riding Stables (Area 5)
Sue Benbow, Selattyn, Oswestry, SY10 7NZ, United Kingdom
01691 718406
sue@springhillfarm.co.uk

Squirrells Riding School (Area 11)
Hayley Squirell,116 Common Road, Blue Bell Hill, ME5 9RG, United Kingdom
01634 681000
i.squirrell@sky.com

St James City Farm and Riding School (Area 9)
Imran Atcha,23 Albany Street, Gloucester, GL1 4NG, United Kingdom
01452208127
imran@thefriendshipcafe.com

St Leonards Equitation Centre (Area 16)
Andrew Reeve, Polston, Launceston, PL15 9QR, United Kingdom
01566 775543
info@stleonardsequestrian.co.uk

St Patricks Way Stables (Area 17)
Sharon Madine, Mearne Road, Downpatrick, BT30 6SY, United Kingdom
07414 922528
stpatrickswaystables@hotmail.co.uk

St Teresa's Equestrian (Area 11)
Alan Miller, St Teresas Equestrian Centre, St Teresas School, Critten Lane, Effingham, RH5 6ST, United Kingdom
01372 750257
equestrian@st-teresas.com

Stag Lodge (Area 11)
Melanie Gatt, Stag Lodge Stables, 197 Robin Hood Way, SW20 0AA, United Kingdom
0208 949 6999
info@staglodgestables.com

Stainsby Grange Equestrian Centre (Area 2)
Paula Allen, Stainsby Grange Equestrian Centre, Thornaby, TS21 9AB, United Kingdom
01642 762233
margaretsouth77@yahoo.co.uk

Stickney Riding Centre (Area 6)
Sharon Poole, Highfield House, Main Road, Stickney, PE22 8AG, United Kingdom
07716 106325
stickneyridingcentre@gmail.com

Stonar School Equestrian Centre (Area 14)
Ellie Halsey, Stonar School, Atworth, Melksham, SN12 8NT, United Kingdom
01225 701766
j.chinn@stonarschool.com

Stourport Riding Centre (Area 7)
Gemma Ash, Hartlebury Road, Stourport, DY13 9JD, United Kingdom
01299 251125
enquiries@stourportridingcentre.co.uk

Summerfield Stables (Area 7)
Georgina Urwin, Brookwood Avenue, Hall Green, Birmingham B28 0DA
07380533118
summerfieldstables96@gmail.com

Sunnybank Equestrian Centre (Area 10)
Terinna Pesci-Griffiths, Sunnybank Equestrian Centre, Rudry Road, Rudry, CF83 3DT, United Kingdom
07767 374079
terinna@sunnybankec.com

Swinhoe Farm Riding Centre (Area 2)
Claire Nixon, Swinhoe Farm House, Belford, NE70 7LJ, United Kingdom
07762 773559
nixonclaire76@hotmail.com

Talygarn Equestrian Centre (Area 10)
Christine Rogers, Talygarn, Pontyclun, Rhondda Cynon Taff, CF72 9JT, United Kingdom
01443 225107
talygarn@googlemail.com

Tandridge Priory Riding Centre (Area 11)
Jo Worsley, Barrow Green Road, Oxted, RH8 9NE, United Kingdom
01883 712863
joworsley51@gmail.com

Tannoch Stables (Area 1)
Dawn Harrison, Palacerigg Road, Cumbernauld, G67 3HU, United Kingdom
01236 733424
enquiries@tannoch.co.uk

Tedworth Equestrian (Area 14)
Pip Lake, Humber Lane, Tidworth, SP9 7AW, United Kingdom
01980 846464
info@tedworthparkriding.com

Tewkesbury Pony Club Centre (Area 9)
Jo Bowen, Cherry Orchard Lane, Twyning, Tewkesbury, GL20 6JH, United Kingdom
07879 027790
info@hillviewlakes.biz

The 4 Gaits Riding School (Area 11)
Lisa Evans, Bullands, Pluckley Road, Smarden TN27 8RQ, United Kingdom
07706 039360
lisaevans307@gmail.com

The Elms (Area 9)
Sarah Hance, The Elms, Colwall, Malvern, WR1 6EF, United Kingdom
Jojo.Glanvill@elmsschool.co.uk

The Leys Riding School (prev. Sea Horse Stables) (Area 1)
Haylie Lawson, Leys of Boysack Farm, Leys Mi DD11 4RT, United Kingdom
01241 830643
haylielawson@hotmail.co.uk

The Owl House Stables (Area 11)
Louise Claringbould, The Owl House, Station Road, St. Margarets-at-Cliffe, Dover, CT15 5LA, United Kingdom
01304 852035
owlstables@aol.com

The Pony Ranch (Area 8)
Josie Allen, The Stables, Lanbrook, St Marys Lane, Hertingfordbury SG14 2LD
07802 214573
theponyranch1@gmail.com

The Stables at Cissbury (Area 11)
Rebecca Hill, Nepcote, Findon, BN14 0SR, United Kingdom
07887 686151
thestables@cissbury.com

The Talland School of Equitation (Area 9)
Pammy and Brian Hutton, Dairy Farm, Ampney Knowle, Cirencester, GL7 5ED, United Kingdom
01285 740155
secretary@talland.net

The Unicorn Centre (Area 2)
Claire Pitt, Stainton Way, Hemlington, TS8 9LX, United Kingdom
01642 576222
enquiries@rdaunicorncentre.co.uk

Throstle Nest Riding School (Area 3)
Jeannette Wheeler, Wilsden Equestrian Centre, Laneside, Wilsden, BD15 0LQ, United Kingdom
07501 257978
wilsdenequestriancentre@gmail.com

Timbertops Equestrian Centre (Area 11)
Jasmine Forsdick, Timbertops Farm, Old Maidstone Road, Sidcup, DA14 5AR, United Kingdom
02083 008506
jasmine.ellis@hotmail.co.uk

Tipton Hall Riding School (Area 9)
Sue Benbow, Cherry Fields, Tedstone, Delamere, Bromyard, HR7 4PR, United Kingdom
01885 488791
sue@tiptonhall.co.uk

Tong Lane End Equestrian Centre (Area 3)
Pamela Crosby, Westgate Hill Street, Bradford, BD4 0SB, United Kingdom
01274 686332 - 07714150103
tleequestriancentre@hotmail.co.uk

Tregoyd Riding Centre (Area 10)
Haydn Jones, Lower Cwmcadarn Farm, Felindre, Three Cocks, LD3 0TB, United Kingdom
01497 847351
tregoydriding@btconnect.com

Trenley Park Liveries (Area 11)
Andrew Payne, The Old Wood Yard, Stodmarsh Road, Fordwich, Canterbury, CT3 4AR, United Kingdom
01227 789179
enquiries@trenley-park.co.uk

Trent Park Equestrian Centre (Area 8)
Sue Martin, East Pole Farmhouse, Bramley Road, N14 4UW, United Kingdom
02083 638630
ponyclub@trentpark.com

Triley Fields Equestrian Centre (Area 10)
Beccy Field, Aberhall Farm, St. Owens Cross, Hereford, HR2 8LL, United Kingdom
01873 890523
trileyponyclubcentre@hotmail.com

Tullymurray Equestrian Centre (Area 17)
Marion Turley,145 Ballyduggan Road, Downpatrick, BT30 8HH, United Kingdom
02844 811880
sarahjgething@aol.com

Tumpy Green Equestrian & Competition Centre (Area 9)
Renee Watkins, Tumpy Green Lane, Cam, Dursley, GL11 5HZ, United Kingdom
01453 899002
info@tumpygreenequestrian.co.uk

Uist Community Riding School (Area 1)
Sue McDonald, Balivanich, Isle of Benbecula, HS7 5LA, United Kingdom
01870 602808
info@ridehebrides.org

Underhill Riding Stables (Area 10)
Kath Bufton, Dolau, Llandrindod Wells, LD1 5TL, United Kingdom
01597 851890
info@underhillridingstables.co.uk

Vale Mill Pony Club Centre (Area 3)
Jackie Butterfield, Vale Mill Lane Stables, Vale Mill Lane, Crossroads, Haworth, BD22 0EF, United Kingdom
01535 649448
info@haworthrda.co.uk

Valley Farm Equestrian Centre Ltd (Area 7)
Denise Faulkner, Mollington Lane, Shotteswell, Banbury, OX17 1HZ, United Kingdom
01295 730576 / 07852
denisefaulkneruk@aol.com

Valley Riding School (Area 11)
Teresa Higgins, Woodhatch Road, Reigate, Redhill RH1 5JJ
07971548294
valleyriding@hotmail.com

Wardhaugh Farm (Area 1)
Julie Thompson, Inverkeithny, Huntly, AB54 7XE, United Kingdom
01466 781803
wardhaughfarm@gmail.com

Wardhouse Equestrian Centre (Area 19)
Ian Couttie, Forehouse Road, Kilbarchan, PA10 2PU, United Kingdom
01505 702565
wardhouse.equestrian@gmail.com

Waterstock Dressage Ltd (Area 12)
Arabella Whelan, Waterstock Pony Club, Waterstock, OX33 1JS, United Kingdom
07711276996
arabella@waterstockdressage.com

Wellgrove Farm Equestrian (Area 11)
Emma Whittaker, Wellgrove Oast, Kings Tol Road, Pembury, TN2 4BE, United Kingdom
01892 822087
enquiries@wellgrovestables.co.uk

Wellington Riding (Area 13)
David Sherin, Basingstoke Road, Heckfield, Hook, RG27 0LJ, United Kingdom
01189 326308
ridinginfo@wellington.co.uk

Wellsfield Equestrian Centre (Area 1)
Julie Harris, Stirling Road, Denny, FK6 6QZ, United Kingdom
01324 820022
enquiries@wellsfield.co.uk

Wester Dowald Equine Centre (Area 1)
Yvonne Campbell, Wester Dowald, Highlandmanloan, PH7 3QU, United Kingdo
07754 596746
westerdowaldequinecentre@yahoo.co.uk

Whiteleaf Riding Stables (Area 11)
Brenda Tyler, Whiteleaf Stables, Lower Road Teynham, Sittingbourne, ME9 9LR, United Kingdom
01795 522512
whiteleafstables@hotmail.co.uk

Wick Riding School (Area 14)
Samantha Pepperall, Wick House, Wick St Lawrence, BS22 7YJ, United Kingdom
01934 515811
samatwick@aol.com

Wickstead Farm Equestrian Centre (Area
Vicki Mace, Eastrop, Highworth, Swindon, S 7PP, United Kingdom
01793 762265
info@wicksteadfarm.co.uk

Widbrook Arabian Stud and Equestrian Centre (Area 14)
Karen Griggs, Old Farm, Widbrook, Trowbridge Road, Bradford on Avon, BA15 1UD, United Kingdom
01225 862 608
enquiry@widbrookequestrian.co.uk

Widmer Equestrian (Area 12)
Jenny Davies, Widmer Farm, Pink Road, Lacey Green, HP27 0PG, United Kingdom
01844 275139
widmerec@hotmail.co.uk

Wildwoods Riding Centre (Area 11)
Anthea Chambers, Wildwoods Riding Centre, Wildwoods, Motts Hill Lane, Walton on the Hill, Tadworth, KT20 5BH, United Kingdom
01737 812146
reception@wildwoodsriding.co.uk

Willington Hall Riding Centre (Area 5)
Sandra Hassett, Willington Road, Willington, Tarporley, CW6 0NA, United Kingdom
01829 751920
info@willingtonriding.co.uk

Willow Farm Riding School (Area 8)
Jane Russell,20 Yarmouth Road, Ormesby St Margaret, Great Yarmouth, NR29 3QE, United Kingdom
07802 607064
m10jor@yahoo.co.uk

Wirral Riding Centre (Area 5)
P Jones, Haddon Lane, Ness, CH64 8TA, United Kingdom
0151 336 3638
phil@wirralridingcentre.com

Witham Villa Riding Centre (Area 7)
Verity Saul, Cosby Road, Broughton Astley, LE9 6PA, United Kingdom
01455 282694
withamvillarc@yahoo.co.uk

Withersfield Hall Equestrian Centre (Area 8)
Marcia Mytton-Mills, Withersfield, Haverhill, CB9 7RY, United Kingdom
01440 702146
marcia.mytton-mills@sky.com

Witherslack Hall Equestrian Centre (Area 4)
Deana Tarr, Witherslack Hall Farm, Witherslack, Grange over Sands, LA11 6SD, United Kingdom
01539 552244
info@whec.co.uk

Woodbine Stables (Area 7)
Sue Ward, Woodbine Farm, Grandborough Fields, Nr Rugby, CV23 8BA, United Kingdom
07908 975164
sue@woodbine-stables.co.uk

Woolacombe Riding Stables (Area 15)
John Middleton, Eastacott Farm, Beach Road, Woolacombe, EX34 7AE, United Kingdom
01271 870260
woolacomberidingstables@btconnect.com

Worcester Riding School and Pony Club Centre (Area 9)
Deni Harper-Adams, Lower Clifton Farm, Clifton, Severn Stoke, WR8 9JF, United Kingdom
07889 569009
denihal@icloud.com

Wrea Green Equitation Centre (Area 4)
Christine Pollitt, Bryning Lane, Bryning, Wrea Green, Nr Kirkham, PR4 3PP, United Kingdom
01772 686576
kidd00@btinternet.com

Yorkshire Riding Centre (Area 3)
Gemma Womersley, Laith Staid Lane, Leeds, LS25 6JU, United Kingdom
07748115588
riding@yorkshireec.co.uk

PONY CLUB INTERNATIONAL ALLIANCE

AUSTRALIA
ponyclubaustralia.com.au

CEO Catherine Ainsworth
ceo@ponyclubaustralia.com.au

Chair Heather Disher
chair@ponyclubaustralia.com.au

CANADA
canadianponyclub.org

Chairman Jane Goodliffe
national_chair@canadianponyclub.org
janegoodliffe@gmail.com

Vice Chairman Naomi Girling
naomi.girling@canadianponyclub.org

Admin Annette Buis
info@canadianponyclub.org

HONG KONG
hongkongponyclub.com

DC Elise McAuley
dc@hongkongponyclub.com

Sec
secretary@hongkongponyclub.com

NEW ZEALAND
nzpca.org

Chair Emma Barker
nzemmabarker@icould.com

CEO Samantha Jones
samantha@nzpca.org

REPUBLIC OF IRELAND
irishponyclub.ie

Chairman Michael Essame
chairman@irishponyclib.ie

Admin Jane Farrell
jane@irishponyclub.ie

SOUTH AFRICA
Chairman Cecile Watt
cecilewatt@mweb.co.za

UNITED STATES OF AMERICA
ponyclub.org

President Ben Duke
bend@ponyclub.org

Exec Director Teresa Woods
executivedirector@ponyclub.org

Intl Liaison Sue Smith
cedarbank.shs@gmail.com

EURO PONY CLUB

AUSTRIA
Gillian Schorn
gill.schorn@gps@aon.at

BELGIUM
Anne Depiesse
secretariat@ffe.be

FRANCE
Tania Melikian
tania.melikian@ffe.com

GERMANY
Maria Schierhoelter-Otte

HUNGARY
Eszter Kovacs (Secretary & Board Member)
keszter@poniklub.hu

IRELAND
Sylvaine Galligan (Treasurer & Board Member)
sylvainegalligan@gmail.com

ITALY
Mrs Christofolettis
info@scuderiadellacapinera.it
alexvirgolici@yahoo.com

LEBANON
Carla Katouah
ck@equisystem.info

NETHERLANDS
Marinus Vos
mjvos@freeler.nl

POLAND
Antony Chlapowski
info@centrumhipiki.com

ROMANIA
Vadim Virgolici (Vice-President & Board Member)
mschierhoelter@fn-dokr.de

SPAIN
Rafael Villalòn Gòmez
rafa@escuelahipicalaespuela.es

SWEDEN
Margareta Wetterberg (President & Board Member)
margareta.wetterburg@telia.com

TURKEY
Tulya Kurtulan
tulya@t-ask.org.tr

UK
Angela Yeoman (Board Member)
ayeoman@btinternet.com

OVERSEAS PONY CLUB CENTRES

OVERSEAS CENTRE COORDINATOR

Rosemary Clarke
overseas.centres@pcuk.org
07729 016978

BAHRAIN

Twin Palms Riding Centre
Oliver Walter, Twin Palms Riding Centre, RD2542, Block 252, Saar, Bahrain, RD2542
ponyclub@twinpalmsridingcentre.com

CAYMAN ISLANDS

Cayman Riding School
Tracey Surrey, Cayman Riding School, Hirst Road, Savannah Newlands, Grand Cayman
caymanridingschool@gmail.com
caymanridingschool.business.site

Equestrian Centre of the Cayman Islands
Mary Alberga, Equestrian Centre of the Cayman Islands, PO Box 818, Grand Cayman, KY1 1103
equestriancentercayman@gmail.com

CHINA

Equuleus International Riding Club
Michelle Wang, Equuleus International Riding Club, No. 91, Shun Bai Road, Cuigezhuang County, Chao Yang District, Beijing, China, 100102
ponyclub@equriding.com
equriding.com

JAMAICA

Caymanas Pony Club
Heidi Lalor, Caymanas Pony Club, Caymanas Estate,
Kingston, Jamaica
hlalor@icwi.com
caymanasponyclub.com

SINGAPORE

Bukit Timah Saddle Club
Bukit Timah Saddle Club, 51 Fairways Drive, Singapore, 286965
ponyclub@btsc.org.sg
btsc.org.sg

SUDAN

Khartoum International Community Scho
Khartoum International Community School
PO Box 1840, Khartoum, Sudan
kics.sd

SWITZERLAND

Bonnie Ponies
Pia Stettler, Bonnie Ponies, Hinterauli 4, CH-8492 Wila
contact@bonnieponies.ch
bonnieponies.ch

UAE

Al Habtoor Polo Resort and Club
Al Habtoor Polo Resort and Club, Al Habtoo Riding School, Dubai Land, Behind the Villa, Dubai, UAE, PO Box 32304
ridingschool@alhabtoorpoloclub.com

Al Marmoom Equestrian Club
Yana Shuhaylo, Al-Marmoom Equine Thera
Al Qudra Road, Al Marmoom Area, Dubai, U
PO Box 939788
info@marmoom.net
marmoom.net

Desert Palm Riding Centre
Desert Palm Riding Centre, Dubai Polo and Equestrian Club, After Dragon Mart 2, 2nd right, Al Warsan 2nd, Dubai Hatta Road, Dub UAE
ridingschool@desertpalmllc.com

Emirates Equestrian Centre

Emirates Equestrian Centre, P.O.Box 292,
Dubai, UAE
dubaiponyclub@emiratesequestriancentre.
com
emiratesequestriancentre.com

Sharjah Equestrian

Annie Haresign, Interchange #6, Al Dhaid
Road, Al Atain, Sharjah, PO Box 1991, United
Arab Emirates
aharesign@yahoo.co.uk
serc.ae

INDEX

Printed in Great Britain
by Amazon

12998319R00075